Fundamental Science in English II

S SEIBIDO

音声ファイルのダウンロード／ストリーミング

CD マーク表示がある箇所は、音声を弊社 HP より無料でダウンロード／ストリーミングすることができます。トップページのバナーをクリックし、書籍検索してください。書籍詳細ページに音声ダウンロードアイコンがございますのでそちらから自習用音声としてご活用ください。

https://www.seibido.co.jp

Fundamental Science in English II

は　し　が　き

　本書「Fundamental Science in English Ⅱ」は、理工系学生のための英語教科書「Fundamental Science in English」シリーズの第2弾です。前書「Fundamental Science in English I」が小・中学校レベルの「数学（算数）」「理科」の内容を扱っていたのに対し、本書は中学校から高等学校レベルの数学・理科の内容をもとに書かれているという違いがありますが、その理念、つまり学習者がすでに（英語以外の）授業で習ったことをあらためて英語で読んだり書いたりできるようになるための教科書であるということに変わりはありません。

　この教科書で英語を学ぶ皆さんは、数学や物理、化学などの授業で、すでに「三角関数」や「元素」、「力」、などについて学んだ記憶があるはずです。そのときに「これは英語ではどう表現するのだろう？」と思ったことはありませんか。もしそう思ったことがあるのなら、この教科書を使って英語を学ぶことは文字通り「一石二鳥」の学習となることでしょう。なぜなら、この教科書で英語を学ぶ皆さんにとって、このような数学や理科の内容はそれほど遠い記憶ではないはずですし、あらためてそれらの内容を英語で学び直すことで、理工系学生にとって必須の数学や物理、化学などの内容の復習と、それらを英語で表現するスキルを新たに獲得できるからです。

　前書の「はしがき」にも書いた通り、理工系の学生諸君は、近い将来に実験レポートや研究論文を英語で読んだり書いたりすることや、海外の学生や研究者たちと英語でディスカッションしたりすることが必須となります。そしてそのための第一歩として、自然科学に関する基本的な内容を英語で読み、またそれらを英語で表現することは、とても有益な練習になることでしょう。

　本書の出版にあたって、この企画に賛同いただき、発行にご尽力いただいた、株式会社成美堂の佐野英一郎社長ならびに同社編集部の田村栄一、宍戸貢両氏に、この場をお借りしてお礼申し上げます。

2019 年 3 月

亀山太一

基本的な文法の復習 (Fundamental Science in English I より抜粋)

● 品詞について

英単語は、それが文の中でどのような意味や役割を持っているかによっていくつかの種類に分けられます。この分類を**品詞**といいます。下の表は、英語を学ぶのに必要不可欠な主な品詞を一覧にまとめたものです。

品詞名	役割	例	解説
名詞	「もの」や「こと」を表す語	water, sky, [a white dog]	**[a white dog]** のように2語以上の単語が集まって1つの名詞を表すものを「名詞句」という。
代名詞	名詞の代わりをする語	I, he, something, nothing,	**人称代名詞**は文の中でどのような役割をするかによって形が変わる。これを**格変化**という（下の表を参照）。
形容詞	名詞の状態や様子を説明する語	big, white, old	分詞や関係詞などを使って形容詞の働きをする語句（形容詞句）を作ることもできる。
助動詞	動詞の前に置いて、動詞の意味を補足する語	do (does), did, can, should	進行形や受動態を作るbeや、完了形のhaveも助動詞とみなすことができる。
動詞	動作や状態を表す語	be, run, know, give, make	時制（過去、進行、完了）や態（受動態）によって過去形、現在・過去分詞形などの活用形が使われる。
副詞	動詞、形容詞、文など、名詞以外の語句を説明する語	sometimes, quickly, [every day], [for the first time]	2語以上の単語が集まって「副詞句」を作ることが多い。副詞(句)は、「いつ」「どこで」「どのように」「なぜ」などを説明する。
前置詞	名詞の前に置いて形容詞句、副詞句を作る語	in, from, between, through	形容詞句になる例： 　The book [on the desk] is mine. 副詞句になる例： 　A cat is sleeping [on the bed].
接続詞	2つ以上の単語（語句）や文をつなぐ語	and, or, if, but, when	接続詞は、**名詞**と**名詞**、**文**と**文**のように、同じ性質の語句・文をつなぐ。

※品詞は、その語が文の中でどのような使われ方をしているかによって決まるものなので、同じ単語でも使われ方によって品詞が変わる場合があります。例えば、Tomorrow is my birthday. の tomorrow は**名詞**、I go to school tomorrow. の tomorrow は**副詞**です。

人称代名詞の格変化

	一人称		二人称	三人称			
	単数	複数	単数/複数	単数			複数
主格	I	we	you	he	she	it	they
所有格	my	our	your	his	her	its	their
目的格	me	us	you	him	her	it	them
独立所有格（所有代名詞）	mine	ours	yours	his	hers	its	theirs

● 文型について

　英語の文は、動詞を中心にした語順によって意味が決まり、語の配列パターンは大きく分けると下のような5つに分けられます。このパターンのことを**文型**といいます。

① **(S + V)**

S（主語）	V（述語動詞）	〔M（修飾語句）〕
Kenji	goes	to a technical school.

② **(S + V + C)**

S（主語）	V（述語動詞）	C（補語）	〔M（修飾語句）〕
My brother	will become	a high school student	next year.

※この文型では「S = C（SはCだ）」という関係になる。

③ **(S + V + O)**

S（主語）	V（述語動詞）	O（目的語）	〔M（修飾語句）〕
Ken	is playing	baseball	with his friends.

④ **(S + V + O₁ + O₂)** $(S + V + O_1 + O_2)$

S（主語）	V（述語動詞）	O_1（目的語）	O_2（目的語）	〔M（修飾語句）〕
Ms. Tanaka	teaches	us	English	every week.

⑤ **(S + V + O + C)**

S（主語）	V（述語動詞）	O（目的語）	C（補語）	〔M（修飾語句）〕
They	named	the baby	Taro	when he was born.

※この文型では「**O = C（OはCだ）**」という関係になる。

　S（主語）、**V**（述語動詞）、**O**（目的語）、**C**（補語）の4つを「**文の要素**」といいます。平叙文においては、文の要素の順序が入れ替わることはありません。疑問文や感嘆文など、平叙文を変形して作られる文では、これらの要素の順序が変わります。

　M（修飾語句）は**副詞句**（節）で、これは文の要素には含まれず、その位置も厳密には決まっていません。修飾語句が文頭に来たり、述語動詞の前後に置かれたりすることもあります。文型を考えるときは、修飾語句は除いて考えます。

文型を理解するために覚えておくとよいルール

　S（主語）と**O**（目的語）は、必ず**名詞**（句）。

　C（補語）は、**名詞**（句）または**形容詞**（句）。

　助動詞がある場合は、それも**V**（述語動詞）に含まれる。

　①②の文型で述語動詞に使われる動詞（目的語のない動詞）を**自動詞**という。

　③④⑤の文型で述語動詞に使われる動詞（後に必ず目的語がある動詞）を**他動詞**という。

疑問文の語順

1) 平叙文に含まれる**述語動詞**（前ページ参照）の中の**助動詞**を主語の前に移動します。

2) 一般動詞の**現在形**、**過去形**は、**助動詞の do (does), did** と**動詞の原形**が結びついたものだと考えます。

 (does + have → has   does + equal → equals   did + go → went)

 He can speak English well.

 → Can he speak English well?

 This school has (= does have) 1,000 students.

 → Does this school have 1,000 students?

※ **述語動詞**が **be 動詞**の場合は、その **be 動詞**を主語の前に移動します。

 That boy is a high school student.

 → Is that boy a high school student?

関係代名詞（制限用法：主格）

関係代名詞を使って名詞を後置修飾することを**関係代名詞**の**制限用法**といいます。**関係代名詞**によって修飾される名詞を**先行詞**といい、「**先行詞＋関係詞節**」が一つの**名詞節**としてはたらきます。

 (Here is) *a polygon*. ← **It** has four sides.

先行詞となる語（polygon）が後の文中で主格（**it**）になっているので、**主格**の関係代名詞 **that** を使って、

 (Here is) [*a polygon* that has four sides]. とします。

関係代名詞（制限用法：所有格）

 (Here is) *a polygon*. ← **Its** sides are all the same length.

先行詞となる語（polygon）が後の文中で所有格（**its**）になっているので、**所有格**の関係代名詞 **whose** を使って、

 (Here is) [*a polygon* whose sides are all the same length]. とします。

関係代名詞（制限用法：目的格）

 (The area of a figure means the number of) *unit squares*. ← The figure contains **them**.

先行詞となる語（unit squares）が説明文中で目的格（**them**）になっているので、目的格の関係代名詞**that**を使って、

 (The area of a figure means the number of) [*unit squares* **that** the figure contains]. とします。

- **主格**の関係代名詞は、先行詞が［人］である場合は**who**、［もの］である場合は**that**または**which**が使われます。
- **所有格**の関係代名詞は先行詞にかかわらず**whose**を使います。
- **目的格**の関係代名詞は、**主格**の場合と同じく、先行詞が［人］である場合は**who (whom)**、［もの］である場合は**that**または**which**が使われます。

関係代名詞（非制限用法）

「**先行詞＋関係詞節**」が一つの名詞句を作る**関係代名詞の制限用法**に対し、主節をコンマ（,）で区切った後に関係詞節を続ける使い方を**関係代名詞の非制限用法（継続用法）**といいます。この用法での関係詞節は先行詞を修飾するのではなく、主節を補足的に説明する文のような役割をします。

 A regular triangle has *three angles,* **which** are all 60 degrees.

非制限用法の場合、関係代名詞は「**接続詞＋代名詞**」で書き換えることができます。

 A regular triangle has *three angles,* **and they** are all 60 degrees.

非制限用法の関係詞節が文の途中に挿入されることもあります。

 A square, **which** is one of the regular polygons, has equal sides and angles.

関係代名詞の**that**には非制限用法はないので使えません。

修飾する先行詞を持たず、**what**以下の関係詞節が「〜する**もの・こと**」という意味の名詞節になります。

関係代名詞の**what**は、関係詞節の中で①**主格的**に使われる場合と②**目的格的**に使われる場合があります。

① (The stars belong to) *X*. ← **X** is called the Milky Way Galaxy.

　　　　　　　　↑
　　　　特定の先行詞がないのでXとする

　Xをそのまま関係代名詞**what**に替えて、

　(The stars belong to) [**what** is called the Milky Way Galaxy]. とします。

② (*Amanogawa* is) *X*. ← We call **X** the Milky Way in English.

　　　　　↑
　　特定の先行詞がないのでXとする

　Xを関係代名詞**what**に替えて前に出し、

　(*Amanogawa* is) [**what** we call the Milky Way in English]. とします。

関係副詞

関係代名詞と同じく、名詞を**後置修飾**します。関係代名詞との違いは、説明文の中で先行詞が**副詞句**の一部になっていることです。つまり、先行詞が「場所」や「時」、「原因・理由」、「方法」などを表す名詞であるとき、これを後置修飾する関係詞節を**関係副詞**を使って作ります。

　(The origin is) *the point*. ← The two axes cross **there** (= **at the point**).

先行詞となる語 (the point) が後の文中で場所を表す副詞 (**there**) に含まれるので、場所を表す関係副詞**where**を使って、

　(The origin is) [*the point* where the two axes cross]. とします。

　[*The country* where the largest number of people live] is China.

関係副詞の非制限用法

関係代名詞と同じように、**関係副詞**も**非制限用法**で使うことができます。

One is through ***the lungs*, where** it takes in oxygen and releases carbon dioxide.

「**前置詞＋関係代名詞**」についても、同じように非制限用法で使うことができます。

White blood cells work as part of ***the immune system*, in which** they protect your body against infectious organisms and foreign substances.

Contents

Trigonometry

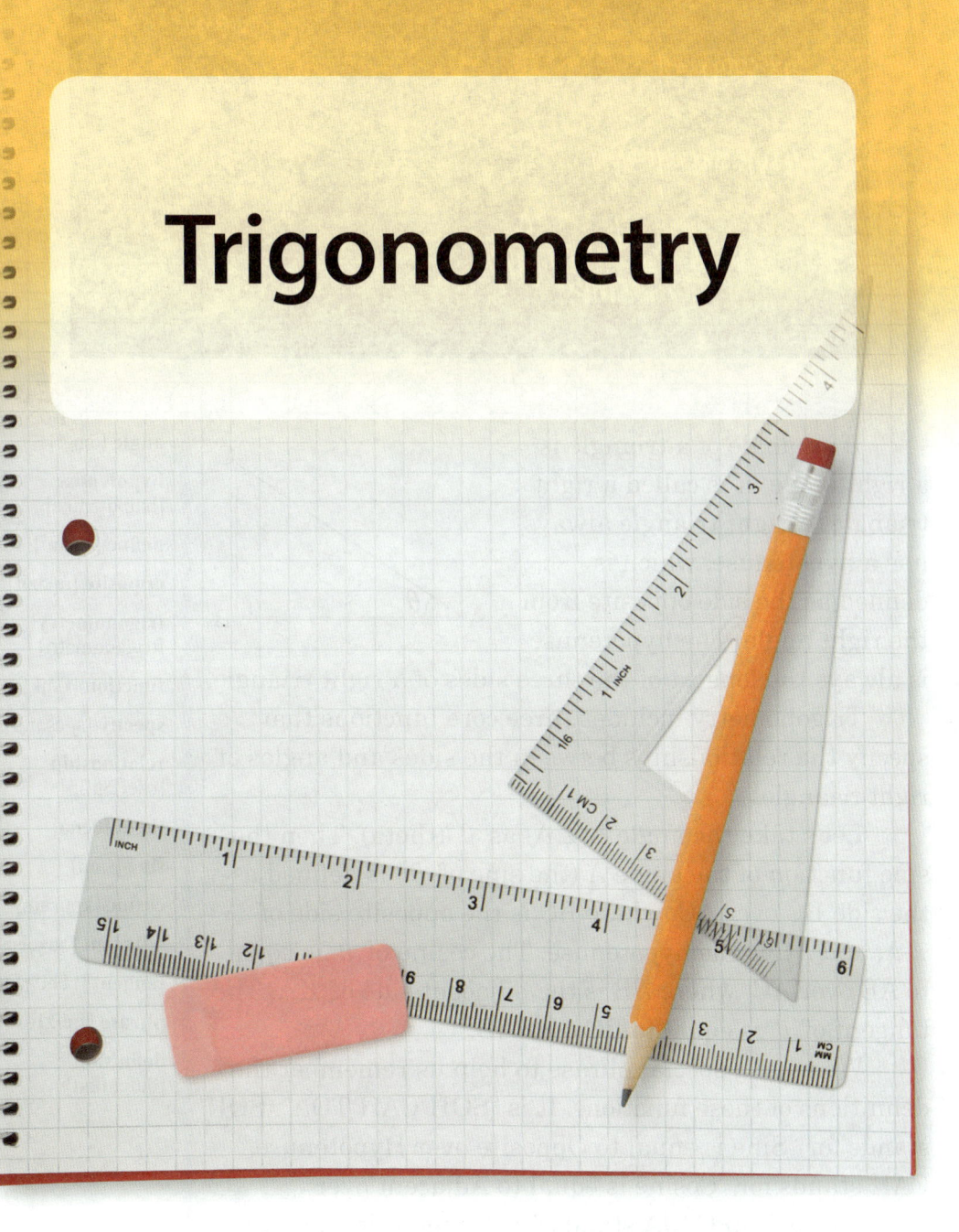

Trigonometric Ratios

CD
1-02~06

If an angle of a triangle is a right angle, it is called a right triangle. A right triangle always has a hypotenuse, which is

5 defined as the side opposite from the right angle. The hypotenuse is always the longest of the three sides of a right triangle.

Trigonometry includes three core functions that specify the relationships between the sides and angles of

10 right triangles.

Let's take the angle A(∠A) as θ (theta). Then the sine function of the angle A (the sine of θ) is defined as the side BC over AC, where BC is the opposite side of ∠A, and AC is the hypotenuse. The cosine of θ is equal

15 to AB over AC, where AB is the adjacent side of ∠A. The tangent of θ is equal to BC over AB.

We have a special phrase to help us remember the definitions of these functions. It is "SOH CAH TOA". SOH stands for "Sine is equal to Opposite over Hypotenuse,"

20 CAH stands for "Cosine is equal to Adjacent over Hypotenuse," and TOA stands for "Tangent is equal to Opposite over Adjacent."

angle [ǽŋgl]

hypotenuse [haipátənùːs]

define [difáin]

opposite [ápəzit]

trigonometry [trìgənámətri]

function [fʌ́ŋkʃən]

specify [spésəfài]

relationship [riléiʃənʃip]

theta [θéitə]

sine [sáin]

cosine [kóusain]

adjacent [ədʒéisənt]

tangent [tǽndʒənt]

phrase [fréiz]

definition [dèfəníʃən]

trigonometric ratio：三角比

🄰🄱🄲 Grammar and Expressions

「代表」を表す不定冠詞a/an （→ p. 8）

A **right triangle** always has a hypotenuse.

「前提条件」を表す where （→ p. 9）

The sine function of the angle A is defined as the side BC over AC, **where** BC is the opposite side of ∠ A, and AC is the hypotenuse.

📑 Practice

Ⓐ 日本語と同じ意味になるように、（　　）内に適切な語を入れましょう。

1. 長方形の4つの角はすべて直角である。

 The four (　　) of a (　　) are all (　　) (　　).

2. ある数と0との積は常に0である。

 The (　　) of any number and zero (　　) (　　) zero.

3. 実数は整数、小数、分数を含んでいる。

 Real numbers (　　) integers, (　　) and (　　).

4. NASAとはアメリカ航空宇宙局の略である。

 NASA (　　) (　　) the National Aeronautics and Space Administration.

5. これらの文章は会社と労働者の関係を規定している。

 These sentences (　　) the (　　) (　　) the company and its employees.

Ⓑ 日本語と同じ意味になるように、[　　]内の語句を並べ替えて言ってみましょう。

1. 彼は私がこの模型飛行機を作るのを手伝ってくれた。

 [he / make / me / helped / model / plane / this].

2. この直線の傾きは、x分のyと定義される。

 [as / defined / is / the / slope / of / over / this / line / y / x].

Ⓒ 1〜2の各文をもとに、関係詞を用いて日本語と同じ意味の英文を作りましょう。

1. A right triangle always has a hypotenuse. It is the longest of its three sides.

 → 直角三角形には必ず斜辺があり、それは3つの辺のうちで一番長い。

2. A regular triangle is a triangle. It has three equal sides.

 → 正三角形とは、3つの等しい長さの辺を持つ三角形である。

Part 2 Radians

Most people are used to the idea of measuring angles in degrees. However, this is not the only way to measure or express the measurement of angles.

In a circle like the figure below, the distance
5 between the center and an arbitrary point on the circumference is called the radius. An arc of a circle is a "portion" of the circumference of the circle.

Let's construct an angle θ (theta) so that the arc that subtends the
10 angle is the same as the radius of the circle in length. In this case, the measurement of the angle θ is defined as 1 radian. In other words, if an angle at the center of a circle is
15 1 radian, the length of the arc that subtends the angle is equal to the radius.

Based on this definition, what will 360 degrees be in terms of radians?

The arc that subtends the angle 360 degrees is the
20 entire circumference. As the length of the circumference is twice the radius times *pi*, 360 degrees is 2π radians.

$\theta = 1$ rad

radian [réidiən]

measure [méʒər]

degree [digríː]

express [iksprés]

measurement [méʒərmənt]

figure [fígjər]

distance [dístəns]

arbitrary [áːrbətrèri]

circumference [sərkʌ́mfərəns]

radius [réidiəs]

arc [áːrk]

portion [póːrʃən]

construct [kənstrʌ́kt]

subtend [səbténd]

entire [entáiər]

1-07~12

---

be used to 〜：〜に慣れている   **in other words**：言い換えれば
based on 〜：〜に基づいて   **in terms of** 〜：〜を単位として

4

ABC Grammar and Expressions

> **so that + S + V ～（～になるように／～できるように）** (→ p. 9)
>
> Let's construct an angle θ **so that** the arc that subtends the angle is the same as the radius of the circle in length.

> **倍数表現** (→ p. 9)
>
> The length of the circumference is **twice** the radius times *pi*.

> **範囲・限定を表す in（～の点において）** (→ p. 10)
>
> The arc that subtends the angle is the same as the radius of the circle **in** length.

Practice

A 日本語と同じ意味になるように、（　　）内に適切な語を入れましょう。

1. 学生たちはコンピューターで文書を作成することに慣れている。

   The students (　　) (　　) (　　) creating documents on the computer.

2. この公式がその方程式の解を得るための唯一の方策というわけではない。

   This formula is (　　) (　　) (　　) (　　) (　　) find the solution of the equation.

3. その間の角が60度になるように、2本の直線を描きなさい。

   Draw two lines (　　) (　　) the angle between them is 60 degrees.

4. 三角形の面積は底辺×高さの半分です。

   The (　　) of a triangle is (　　) the (　　) times (　　).

5. その車はアメリカドルではいくらになりますか。

   How much (　　) the car cost (　　) (　　) (　　) U.S. dollars?

B 日本語と同じ意味になるように、[　　]内の語句を並べ替えて言ってみましょう。

1. 角 θ に対応する円弧はどれですか。

   [angle θ / arc / subtends / the / which]?

2. 次の方程式を x について解きなさい。

   [equation / following / in / of / solve / the / terms / x].

Part 3

Graph of the Sine Function

1-13~17

When you draw a circle with a radius of 1 around the origin of a coordinate plane, it is called a unit circle.

5　　If you draw a line from the center of the circle, it intersects at one point on the circumference of the circle, making a right triangle whose hypotenuse is 1 in length.

10　　Given that the coordinates of the intersection P are (x, y) and the angle between the line OP and the x-axis is θ, the y-coordinate of P will be the sine of θ.

When θ is zero, the y-coordinate of P, which is the sine of θ, is zero. The value of the y-coordinate increases as θ increases, and when θ is 90°, the value of the y-coordinate will be the maximum, which is 1. When θ is more than 90°, the value of the $\sin \theta$ decreases toward zero until θ reaches 180°. The graph of the sine function continues as in the figure below. The shape of the graph is called a sine curve.

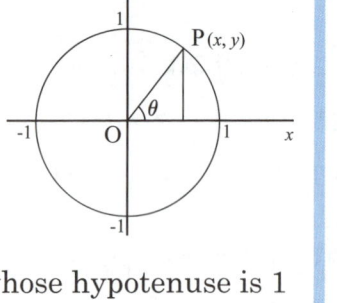

origin [ɔ́(ː)ridʒin]

coordinate [kouɔ́ːrdənit]

plane [pléin]

intersect [ìntərsékt]

intersection [ìntərsékʃən]

axis [ǽksis]

value [vǽljuː]

increase [inkríːs]

maximum [mǽksəməm]

decrease [dìːkríːs]

toward [tɔ́ːrd]

reach [ríːtʃ]

shape [ʃéip]

curve [kə́ːrv]

---

unit circle：単位円　**given that** 〜：〜だと仮定すると、〜ということを考慮すると

Grammar and Expressions

> **変動する数量につく不定冠詞 a/an** (→ p. 8)
>
> When you draw a circle with **a** radius of 1 around the origin of a coordinate plane, it is called a unit circle.

> **「情報共有」を表す定冠詞 the** (→ p. 8)
>
> If you draw a line from the center of **the** circle, it intersects at one point on the circumference of **the** circle.

> **分詞構文** (→ p. 10)
>
> It intersects at one point on the circumference of the circle, **making** a right triangle.

Practice

A 次の（　）内のうち正しいものを選びましょう。

1. (A, The) right triangle has (a, the) right angle.
2. (An, The) area of this figure is (a, the) same as that one.
3. We couldn't see (a, the) moon at (a, the) night.
4. Europa is (a, the) moon of Jupiter.
5. This triangle has (an, the) area of 10 cm^2.
6. (A, The) distance between (a, the) center and (a, the) point on (a, the) circle is constant.

B 日本語と同じ意味になるように、（　）内に適切な語を入れましょう。

1. その関数のグラフはx軸と60度の角をなして交わる。

   The graph of the function (　　　) x-axis (　　　) an angle of 60 degrees.
2. $x - 2 = 0$ であるとしたら、xの値は何ですか。

   (　　　) (　　　) $x - 2 = 0$, what is the (　　　) of x?
3. この角の大きさはラジアンではいくつですか。

   What is this angle (　　　) (　　　)?
4. 直角三角形には斜辺があり、それは3つの辺のうちで最も長い。

   (　　　) right triangle has (　　　) (　　　), (　　　) is the longest of its three sides.

「代表」を表す不定冠詞 a/an

不定冠詞 a/an は、単に「一つの」という意味を表すだけでなく、その名詞が表す事物の「代表」であることを意味することがあります。

　　A **right triangle** always has a hypotenuse.
　　（直角三角形には必ず斜辺がある）◀ 斜辺のない直角三角形はない

上の例文は、直角三角形の性質を表す文であり、この文で述べられている内容は、その名詞で表されるもの（ここでは直角三角形）すべてにあてはまります。これに対し、下のような**冠詞のつかない複数形名詞**の場合は、「一般的にはそうであるが、あてはまらない場合もある」という点で、上の**不定冠詞＋単数名詞**の場合と異なります。

　　Dogs are man's best friends.
　　（犬は人間の最良の友である）◀ そうでない犬もいる

変動する数量につく不定冠詞 a/an

数量を表す名詞で、それが変動するものである場合、その名詞には原則として**不定冠詞 a/an** がつきます。下の例文で、speed, height はいずれも変動（変化）する値を表す名詞なので、ここでは**不定冠詞**がつきます。

- The car is moving at **a speed** of 100 km/h.
  （その車は時速 100 キロで走っている）
- The balloon reached **a height** of 500 meters above the ground.
  （気球は地上 500 メートルの高さに達した）

「情報共有」を表す定冠詞 the

定冠詞 the（＋名詞） の用法として、その名詞が表す「もの」の存在が話し手（書き手）と聞き手（読み手）との間で共有されていることを示すということがあります。下の例文では、最初に **Draw a circle...**（円を描きなさい）と言っているので、文末の**circle**はその描かれた円であるということが理解（情報共有）されるため、**定冠詞 (the)** がつきます。

　　Draw **a circle**, then draw a line from the center of **the circle**.
　　（円を描き、その円の中心から直線を引きなさい）

「前提条件」を表す where

非制限用法の関係副詞 whereは、通常は場所を表す名詞を受けて「そこ（その場所）で〜」という意味を表すことが多いのですが、理工学系の文章ではよく**前提条件**を表す場合に使われます。非制限用法で用いるので、where の前に必ずコンマが必要であることに注意しましょう。

The sine function of the angle A is defined as the side BC over AC, <u>**where**</u> BC is the opposite side of $\angle$ A, and AC is the hypotenuse.
（角 A のサイン関数は辺 AC 分の BC と定義される。<u>ただし</u> BC は角 A の対辺、AC は斜辺とする）

so that + S + V 〜（〜になるように／〜できるように）

so that に続く節は、主節の内容に対してその**目的**や**条件**を表します。

- Let's construct an angle θ <u>**so that**</u> the arc that subtends the angle is the same length as the radius of the circle. （その角に対する弧が円の半径と同じ長さになるように角 θ を取りましょう）
- Let me give you my e-mail address <u>**so that**</u> you can contact me any time. （いつでも連絡できるように私のメールアドレスをお教えします）
- We must rewrite the program <u>**so that**</u> the results can be found faster. （もっと速く結果が出せるようにプログラムを書き換えなければならない）

倍数表現

「〜は…の○倍である」「…の○倍〜する」のような倍数表現は、**倍数＋比較対象となる名詞**で表します。

- The circumference of a circle is <u>**twice**</u> the radius times *pi*. （円周は半径×π の 2 倍である）
- Jet planes fly <u>**ten times**</u> the speed of cars. （ジェット機は自動車の 10 倍の速さで飛ぶ）

twice や **ten times** は副詞（句）であり、上の例文ではそれぞれ **twice** (as long as) the radius times *pi*, **ten times** (as fast as) the speed of cars が省略されたものであると考えるとわかりやすいでしょう。

範囲・限定を表す in（～の点において）

前置詞 **in** は、場所を表すだけでなく、**in + 数量名詞** の形でも多く使われ、数量関係を表す表現や具体的な数値の直後に置かれます。寸法を表す数量名詞には、width（幅）、height（高さ）、depth（深さ、奥行き）、length（長さ）、thickness（厚み）などがあります。

- The metal pipe is 2 kg **in weight** and 5 cm **in diameter**.
  （その金属管は重量が 2 キロ、直径が 5 センチです）

また、以下の例のように、**in + 名詞** がその前の名詞の属性を表すこともあります。

- The difference **in price** is due to the difference **in cost** of materials.
  （値段の違いは材料費の違いによるものである）

分詞構文

分詞（現在分詞、過去分詞） を使って、主節に従属する副詞句を作るのが **分詞構文** です。多くの場合、分詞構文は、接続詞を用いた副詞節を簡略化したものと考えることができ、主節との意味関係が文脈から明らかな場合に使われます。

- **As** he **was** sick, he could not go to school.
  - → **Being** sick, he could not go to school.
    （病気だったので、彼は学校へ行けなかった）
- **When** the sun and the moon **are seen** from the earth, they look almost the same size.
  - → **Seen** from the earth, the sun and the moon look almost the same size.（地上から見ると、太陽と月はほぼ同じ大きさに見える）

分詞構文は文末で使われることもあります。

- A typhoon hit the area, **and** it **caused** serious damage.
  - → A typhoon hit the area, **causing** serious damage.
    （台風がその地域を襲い、甚大な被害をもたらした）
- They **used** simple tools **and** built a small house.
  - → They built a small house **using** simple tools.
    （かれらは簡単な道具を用いて小さな家を建てた）

分詞構文内の動詞の意味上の主語が主節の主語と異なる場合、分詞の直前に主語となる名詞を置きます。この形を **独立分詞構文** といいます。

Because the weather **was** bad, we gave up visiting the garden.
- → **The weather being** bad, we gave up visiting the garden.
  （天気が悪かったので、私たちはその庭園に行くことをあきらめた）

Elements

Periodic Table

Atomic number → **8** | 15.999 ← Atomic weight
O ← Symbol
Oxygen ← Name

Chemistry is a branch of physical science that studies the composition, structure, properties and change of matter

1-18~22

Elements are the smallest units that can no longer be chemically broken down. They are the substances that have specific properties at certain temperatures and react in certain ways. Carbon, calcium and sodium are
5　all elements. Is water an element? No, it's not an element because water can be separated into other elements, hydrogen and oxygen, by electrolysis.

　　Although chemically, elements are the smallest units, they are actually made up of more basic units
10　called atoms. Atoms consist of even more fundamental particles such as protons, neutrons, and electrons.

　　The number of protons in the nucleus of an atom, which is called the atomic number, defines the element. Hydrogen, helium, and carbon have one, two, and six
15　protons respectively. If carbon had seven protons, it would become nitrogen instead of carbon. By definition, if you were somehow to add one proton into a nitrogen atom, it would become oxygen.

　　All known elements can be arranged in order of
20　their atomic numbers as in the chart above. This is called the Periodic Table of Elements.

element [éləmənt]

chemically [kémikəli]

substance [sʌ́bstəns]

specific [spəsífik]

property [prɑ́pərti]

certain [sə́ːrtn]

react [ri(ː)ǽkt]

electrolysis [ilèktrɑ́ləsis]

fundamental [fʌ̀ndəméntəl]

particle [pɑ́ːrtikl]

proton [próutɑn]

neutron [núːtrɑn]

electron [iléktrɑn]

nucleus [núːkliəs]

atomic [ətɑ́mik]

respectively [rispéktivli]

somehow [sʌ́mhàu]

arrange [əréindʒ]

Periodic Table：周期（律）表　**(be) made up of ~**：~からできている
in order of ~：~の順で［に］

Grammar and Expressions

| 仮定法 (1) (→ p. 18)

If carbon **had** seven protons, it **would** become nitrogen instead of carbon.

| no longer ～（もはや～ない） (→ p. 19)

Elements are the smallest units that can **no longer** be chemically broken down.

| if ... be to ～（もし～するならば） (→ p. 19)

If you **were** somehow **to** add one proton into a nitrogen atom, it would become oxygen.

Practice

A 日本語と同じ意味になるように、（　　）内に適切な語を入れましょう。

1. もっと速い計算機があれば、なんとかしてこの複雑な問題が解けるのだが。

If we (　　　) a faster computer, we (　　　) (　　　) solve this complex problem.

2. 正多角形の一辺が他の辺よりも長ければ、定義上それはもう正多角形ではない。

If a side of a regular polygon (　　　) longer than the other, it (　　　)
(　　　) (　　　) (　　　) a regular polygon (　　　) (　　　).

3. この問題を解くには、三角関数が必須です。

If this problem (　　　) (　　　) be solved, trigonometry is essential.

4. ご家族の名前を年齢順に書いてください。

Write down the names of your family (　　　) (　　　) (　　　) age.

B 日本語と同じ意味になるように、［　　］内の語句を並べ替えて言ってみましょう。

1. 炭素とは元素の一つで、化学的にそれ以上分解できない。

Carbon [elements / is / of / one / the], [be / broken / cannot / chemically /
down / which] any more.

2. 水は水素と酸素の原子から成っており、それらは電気分解によって分離することができる。

Water [and / atoms / consists / hydrogen / of / oxygen], [be / by / can /
electrolysis / separated / which].

3. 木星は太陽からの距離の順では5番目の惑星である。

Jupiter is [distance / fifth / from / planet / in / of / order / the / the sun].

Part 2 Isotopes

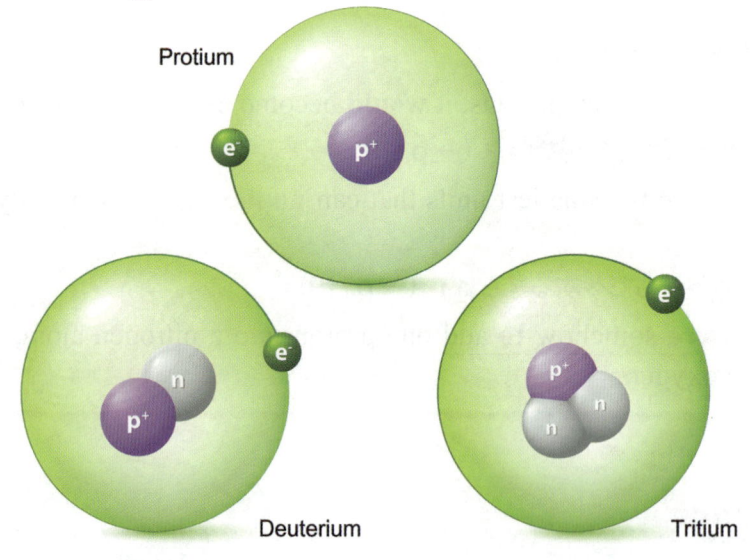

Protium

Deuterium

Tritium

An atom consists of protons, neutrons, and electrons. All atoms of a particular element always have the same number of protons. However, the numbers of neutrons and electrons may differ.

5 Carbon-12, which comprises most of the carbon in the universe, has six protons and six neutrons in the nucleus. Other types of carbon exist that have more than six neutrons. These are called isotopes of carbon.

In addition to carbon, many other elements also
10 have isotopes. Hydrogen, for example, usually has no neutrons. Those with one or two neutrons are called deuterium or tritium respectively, which are isotopes of hydrogen. Isotopes of an element possess the identical chemical properties of their initial elements.

15 The total number of protons and neutrons is called the atomic mass, which identifies what isotope it is. The atomic mass and the atomic number of an isotope are written on the left side of its element symbol. (e.g. $^{12}_{6}C$).

Isotopes that have the same number of protons
20 and neutrons are stable. However, those with a different number of neutrons are often unstable. Some of them emit radiation, transforming themselves into other isotopes. Such isotopes are called radioisotopes.

isotope [áisətòup]

differ [dífər]

comprise [kəmpráiz]

universe [júːnəvə̀ːrs]

exist [igzíst]

possess [pəzés]

identical [aidéntikəl]

initial [iníʃəl]

mass [mǽs]

identify [aidéntəfài]

stable [stéibl]

unstable [ʌnstéibl]

emit [imít]

radiation [rèidiéiʃən]

transform [trænsfɔ́ːrm]

radioisotope [rèidioáisətoup]

1-23~28

carbon-12：炭素 12　deuterium：重水素　tritium：三重水素
atomic mass：原子(質)量　e.g.：例えば

🔤 Grammar and Expressions

間接疑問 (→ p. 18)

The atomic mass identifies **what** isotope it is.
The atomic number defines **what** the element is.

先行する名詞の重複を避ける代名詞 that, those (→ p. 19)

Hydrogen usually has no neutrons. **Those** with one neutron are called deuterium.

📝 Practice

A 2つの英文が同じ意味になるように、( ) 内に適切な語を入れましょう。

1. Both children and adults like this movie.

( ) ( ) children ( ) ( ) adults like this movie.

2. You should learn both English and some other languages.

You should learn ( ) ( ) English ( ) ( ) some other languages.

3. Most snakes don't have legs.

Most snakes have ( ) ( ).

4. He could not buy anything because he didn't have money.

Having ( ) money, he could buy ( ).

B 日本語と同じ意味になるように、[ ] 内の語句を並べ替えて言ってみましょう。

1. 幸福とは何かということを定義することは難しい。

It [define / difficult / happiness / is / is / to / what].

2. 表のそれぞれの数値が何を表しているのか説明してください。

Please explain [each / in / number / represents / the table / what].

3. 鳥の体温は人間の体温よりも5度ほど高い。

A bird's body temperature [about / a human / is / degrees / five / higher / of / than / that].

4. ほとんどの哺乳類は尻尾がある。尻尾のない哺乳類の一つが人間だ。

Most mammals have tails. [humans / are / of / one / no / tails / those / with].

Part 3 Mole

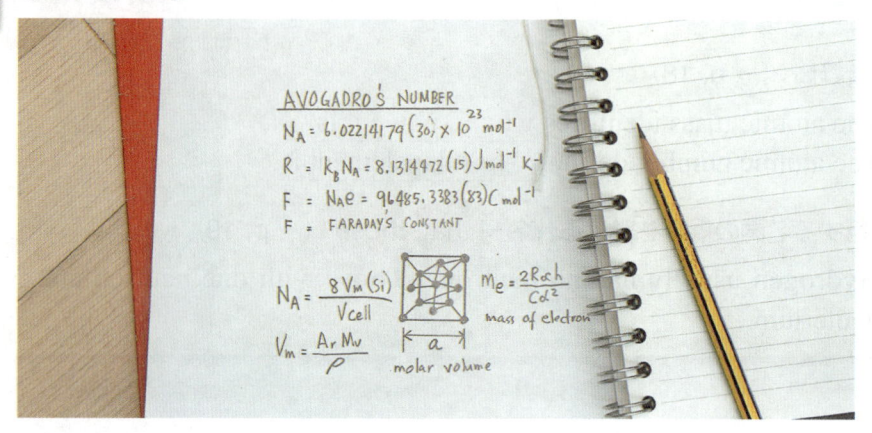

1-29~35

Do you know how to find out how many atoms a substance has? You don't have to worry even if you don't know how to count the number of atoms in a substance one by one. You only have to know the mass in order to
5 find the number of atoms that the substance is comprised of.

For example, 1 gram of hydrogen, regardless of its state such as gas or liquid, is known to contain 6.02×10^{23} hydrogen atoms. This number is called Avogadro's
10 number, which relates the weight to the amount of the elementary entities that comprise the substance. Elementary entities include atoms, molecules, ions and so on.

If a substance is comprised of 6.02×10^{23} atoms or
15 molecules, we say it amounts to 1 mole. Mole is the unit of measurement for the amount of substance, which is symbolized as *mol*.

How much does one mole of water weigh?

As a water molecule consists of two hydrogen atoms
20 whose atomic mass is 1 and one oxygen atom with an atomic mass of 16, one mole of water weighs 18 grams.

Later in the history of chemistry, Avogadro's number was redefined as the exact number of atoms in 12 grams of carbon-12. This is called the Avogadro constant.
25 Even though the definition has been changed, it is still approximated as 6.02×10^{23}.

mole [móul]

regardless [rigá:rdləs]

state [stéit]

gas [gǽs]

liquid [líkwid]

molecule [málǝkjù:l]

relate [riléit]

weight [wéit]

amount [ǝmáunt]

ion [áiǝn]

symbolize [símbǝlàiz]

chemistry [kémistri]

redefine [rìdifáin]

exact [igzǽkt]

constant [kánstǝnt]

approximate [ǝpráksimèit]

....
regardless of 〜：〜にかかわらず　**Avogadro's number**：アボガドロ数　**elementary entities**：
要素粒子　**amount of substance**：物質量　**Avogadro constant**：アボガドロ定数

🔠 **Grammar and Expressions**

> **even if (たとえ〜でも)** (→ p. 20)
>
> You don't have to worry **even if** you don't know how to count the atoms in a substance one by one.
>
> **even though (〜にもかかわらず)** (→ p. 20)
>
> **Even though** the definition has been changed, it is still approximated as 6.02×10^{23}.
>
> **only have to (〜するだけでよい)** (→ p. 20)
>
> You **only have to** know the mass in order to find the number of atoms that the substance is comprised of.

📝 **Practice**

A 次の式を声に出して英語で読みましょう。

1. 6.02×10^{23}
2. 1.3×10^{3}
3. 3.0×10^{-8}
4. $10^{3} \times 10^{4} = 10^{7}$
5. $10^{-5} \times 10^{-6} = 10^{-11}$
6. $10^{m} \times 10^{n} = 10^{m+n}$

B 日本語と同じ意味になるように、（　）内に適切な語を入れましょう。

1. その問題は簡単そうに見えるが、いまだに解明されていない。

   (　　　) (　　　) the problem looks easy, it has not been solved.

2. 空腹であっても、今は何も食べてはいけません。

   You cannot eat anything now (　　　) (　　　) you are hungry.

3. かれらは全員が空腹だったが、何も食べるものがなかった。

   They had nothing to eat (　　　) (　　　) all of them were starving.

4. たとえその惑星に行けたとしても、帰ってくることはできないだろう。

   (　　　) (　　　) you could reach the planet, you (　　　) not be able to return.

5. この問題を解くには、すべての数字を掛け合わせるだけでよい。

   You (　　　) (　　　) (　　　) multiply all the numbers to solve this problem.

6. 食べられるだけ食べても、支払いは1,000円でけっこうです。

   (　　　) (　　　) you eat all you can, you (　　　) (　　　) (　　　) pay 1,000 yen.

仮定法 (1)

仮定法過去は、現在の事実に反して「（実際にはそうではないのだが）もし〜だったら、〜だろう」という仮定や願望を表現（反実仮想表現）するのに使います。

If ＋ S ＋ 述語動詞（過去形）〜，S ＋ would ＋ 動詞（原形）〜.

仮定法過去の文の基本形は、**従属節（if節）内の動詞が過去形**、**主節の述語動詞**は **would ＋ 動詞の原形**という形になります。このように、従属節の動詞が過去形になることから**仮定法過去**と呼ばれますが、決して過去のことについて言っているのではないということに注意してください。例えば下の例文では、「（7個の陽子を持つ炭素というのは存在しないのだが）もし炭素に7個の陽子があったとしたら、それはもはや炭素ではない」という意味になります。

If carbon **had** seven protons, it **would** become nitrogen instead of carbon.

従属節（if節）の動詞が **be動詞**の場合は、主語の人称や数にかかわらず **were** を使うことが一般的です。また、主節の意味や内容によっては、**would** ではなく **could** や **might** を使うこともあります。

If there **were** time machines, we **could** go back in time.（もしもタイムマシンがあれば、私たちは過去に戻ることができるのだが）

仮定法過去が現在の事実に反する仮定をするのに対し、過去の事実に反する仮定をするのに使われるのが**仮定法過去完了**です。仮定法過去完了の文の基本形は、下のように**従属節（if節）内の動詞が過去完了形**、**主節の述語動詞**は **would ＋ have ＋ 動詞の過去分詞**という形になります。

If ＋ S ＋ 述語動詞（過去完了形）〜，S ＋ would ＋ have ＋ 動詞（過去分詞）〜.

下の例文は、「（実際には知らなかったのだが）もし知っていたら〜しただろう」という、過去の事実に反する仮定をしています。

If I **had known** you were sick, I **would have visited** you every day.
（君が病気だと知っていたら、毎日お見舞いに行ったのに）

間接疑問

疑問詞（句）＋ S ＋ V 〜の形になる一連の節が、疑問詞の意味を含む一つの**名詞句**になるものを**間接疑問**といいます。この節の中では、述語動詞は平叙文の形になることに注意しましょう。

• The atomic mass identifies **what** isotope it is.
（原子量によってそれがどんな同位体かがわかる）

- The atomic number defines **what** the element is.
  （原子番号はその元素が何であるかを定義する）
- I don't know **when** he will come back.
  （彼がいつ戻ってくるのか、私にはわかりません）
- The volume of a substance depends on **how fast** the particles move.
  （物質の体積は、粒子がどれだけ速く動くかによって決まる）

なお、疑問詞以外に、**if**（〜かどうか）などの接続詞を使った間接疑問もあります。

I don't know **if** he will come to the meeting tomorrow.
（彼が明日の会議に来るかどうか私は知らない）

先行する名詞の重複を避ける代名詞 that, those

一つの文または連続する複数の文の中で同じ名詞を繰り返して使うのは冗長になるので、前に出た名詞の代わりに代名詞の **that**（複数の場合は **those**）を使うことがよくあります。

- The earth's gravity is greater than **that** of the moon.
  （地球の重力は月のそれ（重力）よりも大きい）
- Hydrogen usually has no neutrons. **Those** with one neutron are called deuterium.（水素は通常は中性子を持たない。1個の中性子を持つそれら（水素）は重水素と呼ばれる）

no longer 〜（もはや〜ない）

否定文で、notなどの否定を表す副詞の代わりに**no longer**を使うと、「もはや〜ない」「それ以上〜ない」という意味を表します。

- You are **no longer** children.（君たちはもう子供じゃない）
- Elements are the smallest units that can **no longer** be chemically broken down.（元素とは、化学的にもうそれ以上分解することができない最小の単位である）

if ... be to 〜（もし〜するならば）

S + be to 〜の構文は「〜することになっている」というのが基本的な意味で、主語の意思が働かない動作を表し、**義務**、**予定**、**運命**、**可能**などを表します。

- The meeting **is to** begin in one hour.（会議は1時間後に始まる予定です）
- Students **are to** bring their own computer to this class.（学生たちはこの授業に自分のコンピューターを持ってくることになっている）

be to 〜の構文を If 節で使うと、「もし〜する（ことになる）としたら」のような意味になります。その場合、実現の可能性が（ほとんど）ない場合は下のように仮定法になります。

- **If** you <u>were to</u> go abroad, which country would you choose?
  （外国へ行くとしたら、どの国を選びますか）
- **If** you <u>were</u> somehow <u>to</u> add one proton into a nitrogen atom, it would become oxygen.（窒素原子になんとかして陽子を 1 個追加できたとしても、それは酸素になってしまう）

even if（たとえ〜でも）

even if ＋「仮定の話」という形で、「たとえ〜でも（…だ）」という意味になります。

You don't have to worry **even if** you don't know how to count the atoms in a substance one by one.（物質中の原子の数を一つひとつ数える方法を知らなくても、心配する必要はありません）

even though（〜にもかかわらず）

though を単独で使った場合とほぼ同じ意味ですが、**even though** の方が意味が強くなります。

- **Though** he is young, he is running a big company.
  （若いけれども、彼は大きな会社を経営している）
- **Even though** he was still young, he became one of the richest people in the world.
  （まだ若かったにもかかわらず、彼は世界の富豪の一人になった）

前の **even if** には「仮定の話」が続くのに対し、**even though** には「事実」が続くということに注意しましょう。

only have to（〜するだけでよい）

have to（〜しなければならない）の前に only を入れることで、「〜するだけでよい」という意味になります。have only to という語順でも同じ意味になります。

You **only have to** know the mass in order to find the number of atoms that the substance is comprised of.（物質を構成している原子の数を知るには、その質量がわかりさえすればよい）

Force

Speed, Velocity and Acceleration

1-36~40

Speed is the rate at which an object moves. When an object has traveled a certain distance in a certain amount of time, its
5 average speed is calculated by dividing the distance by the time.

Velocity is the speed of an object in a particular direction. Such a quantity that has both magnitude and direction is called a vector, while
10 those without direction, like time and speed, are called scalars. When you mention the velocity of an object, you need to state not only the magnitude but also the direction in which the object travels.

The distance-time graph shows the motion of an
15 object. The straight line on the graph shows that the object is traveling at a constant velocity. When the graph runs steep, it means that the object is traveling faster. By contrast, a gentle slope on the graph means the object is traveling more slowly. If the line is horizontal, it means
20 that the object is stationary.

Acceleration is the rate of change in velocity, which is measured in the unit m/s^2. The acceleration can be shown on a
25 velocity-time graph. The gradient of the graph gives the acceleration of the object.

velocity [vəláːsəti]

acceleration [əksèləréiʃən]

rate [réit]

travel [trǽvl]

average [ǽvəridʒ]

calculate [kǽlkjəlèit]

direction [dərékʃən]

quantity [kwántəti]

magnitude [mǽgnətùːd]

vector [véktər]

scalar [skéilər]

mention [ménʃən]

motion [móuʃən]

steep [stíːp]

slope [slóup]

horizontal [hɔ̀(ː)rəzántəl]

stationary [stéiʃənèri]

gradient [gréidiənt]

by contrast：それに対して、一方　**m/s²**：meters per second squared

Grammar and Expressions

前置詞＋関係代名詞　(→ p. 28)

Speed is **the rate at which** an object moves.
You need to state **the direction in which** the object travels.

名詞を強調するsuch　(→ p. 28)

Such a quantity that has both magnitude and direction is called a vector.

「対比」を表すwhile（〜に対し、一方…）　(→ p. 28)

A quantity that has both magnitude and direction is called a vector,
while those without direction are called scalar.

Practice

A 日本語と同じ意味になるように、（　　）内に適切な語を入れましょう。

1. かれらはその音が聞こえてくる方向を見た。
   They looked (　　) the direction (　　) (　　) the sound came.

2. そのロケットが上昇しているときの加速度を求めよ。
   Find the acceleration (　　) (　　) the rocket is rising.

3. 速度の変化の割合が大きいと、グラフの傾きは急になる。
   When the (　　) of (　　) (　　) (　　) is greater, the (　　) of
   the graph is (　　).

B 日本語と同じ意味になるように、［　　］内の語句を並べ替えて言ってみましょう。

1. そんな高速で車を運転してはいけません。
   You can't [a / a car / at / drive / high / speed / such].

2. この本は、三角関数を初めて学ぶという人たちのために書かれました。
   This book [are / for / learn / people / such / to / trigonometry / was / who /
   written] for the first time.

3. 1秒間に10^{15}回計算できるようなコンピューターはスーパーコンピューター
   と呼ばれる。
   [a computer / calculate / can / 10^{15} times / that / per / second / such] is
   called a super computer.

Mass and Forces

CD
1-41~44

Mass is defined as the resistance to acceleration. The greater the mass of an object is, the greater force is needed to change its velocity. If the mass of a stationary object is greater, it is more difficult to move it. You can
5 calculate the force F (N) that gives acceleration of a (m/s^2) to an object whose mass is m (kg) by the formula $F = ma$. This formula is called Newton's equation of motion.

A force is defined as a push or a pull that makes an object change in motion. If the forces acting on an object
10 are balanced, there will be no effect on its movement or velocity. A balanced force lets a stationary object remain stationary, and it lets a moving object continue to move at the same velocity. This is called the law of inertia.

If the forces acting on an object are unbalanced,
15 the velocity of the object will change. Unbalanced forces cause a resultant force, which makes an object change in velocity. The greater the resultant force, the greater the acceleration of the object. If the mass of an object is greater, more force will be needed to cause the same
20 acceleration.

force [fɔ́ːrs]

resistance [rizístəns]

formula [fɔ́ːrmjələ]

equation [ikwéiʒən]

push [púʃ]

pull [púl]

balanced [bǽlənst]

effect [ifékt]

movement [múːvmənt]

remain [riméin]

inertia [inə́ːrʃə]

unbalanced [ənbǽlənst]

resultant [rizʌ́ltənt]

Newton's equation of motion：ニュートンの運動方程式

ABC Grammar and Expressions

形式主語 (→ p. 29)

If the mass of a stationary object is greater, **it** is more difficult **to** move it.

---

the ＋比較級 ～ , the ＋比較級 … (→ p. 29)

（～すればするほど…／～であればあるほど…）

The greater the mass of an object is, **the greater** force is needed to change the velocity.

The greater the resultant force, **the greater** the acceleration of the object.

使役動詞 (→ p. 29)

A force is defined as a push or a pull that **makes** an object change in motion.

A balanced force **lets** a stationary object remain stationary.

📝 Practice

A 日本語の意味に合うよう、次の（　　）内のうち正しいものを選びましょう。

1. 彼の話はいつも私たちを笑わせてくれる。

   His story always (makes, lets) us laugh.

2. 父は自分のパソコンを私に使わせてくれない。

   My father does not (make, let) me use his PC.

3. 電圧を高くするとモーターはより速く回る。

   Higher voltage (makes, lets) the motor turn faster.

4. このアプリで学生たちは楽しく数学を学ぶことができます。

   This application (makes, lets) the students learn math with fun.

B 日本語と同じ意味になるように、（　　）内に適切な語を入れましょう。

1. 高度が高くなればなるほど、かれらが山を登る速さが遅くなった。

   (　　) (　　) the altitude was, (　　) (　　) they climbed the mountain.

2. aの値が大きくなるほどグラフの傾きは急になる。

   (　　) (　　) the (　　) of a, (　　) (　　) the (　　) of the graph.

3. 半径が長いほど、円の面積は大きくなる。

   (　　) (　　) the (　　) of a circle, (　　) (　　) its (　　).

Gravity

CD
1-45~48

Gravity is defined as the force that pulls objects to the ground. The force exerted by gravity onto an object is called its weight. The weight of an object is calculated by multiplying mass by gravitational acceleration. As the
5 earth's gravity is approximately 9.8 m/s², the weight of an object whose mass is 1 kg is 9.8 N, which is also denoted as 1 kgf.

Can you imagine how much you would weigh on the moon? If you stepped onto a scale on the moon, you would
10 weigh much less than your weight on the earth, even though the mass of your body is the same. This is because the gravitational pull of the moon is just about one sixth that of the earth.

Every pair of objects that have mass attract each
15 other by a force called universal gravitation. The force is proportional to the product of the two masses and inversely proportional to the square of the distance between them. Any objects on the earth are attracting with the earth, but the mass of the earth is so much
20 greater. This is why the objects on the earth appear to "fall" to the ground.

gravity [grǽvəti]

exert [igzə́ːrt]

gravitational [grævitéiʃənl]

approximately [əprɑ́ksimətli]

denote [dinóut]

scale [skéil]

attract [ətrǽkt]

universal [jùːnəvə́ːrsəl]

gravitation [grævitéiʃən]

proportional [prəpɔ́ːrʃənəl]

product [prɑ́ːdəkt]

inversely [invə́ːrsli]

appear [əpíər]

....

kgf : kilogram-force

Grammar and Expressions

仮定法 (2) (→ p. 30)

Can you imagine how much you **would** weigh on the moon?

倍数（分数）表現 (→ p. 30)

The mass of the moon is just about **one sixth** that of the earth.

Practice

A 日本語と同じ意味になるように、（　　）内に適切な語を入れましょう。

1. 重力による力が地球上にある物体を地面に向かって引っ張る。
   The ( ) by ( ) pulls objects on the ( ) to the ( ).

2. 1キログラム重とは、質量が1 kgの物体の地球上での重さを意味し、それは9.8 Nである。
   1 kgf ( ) the ( ) of an object ( ) ( ) is 1 kg on the earth, ( ) is 9.8 N.

3. もしあなたが火星で体重計に乗ったら体重はどれくらいでしょうか。
   ( ) ( ) would you ( ) if you ( ) onto a scale on Mars?

4. 火星の重力は地球の重力の約3分の1です。
   The ( ) of Mars is about ( ) ( ) ( ) of the earth.

5. yがxの逆数であるとき、yの値はxに反比例する。
   Given that y is the inverse of x, the ( ) of y is ( ) ( ) ( ) x.

B 本文を参考にして、以下の質問に答える文を作りましょう。

1. What is gravity?
2. What is weight?
3. How is the weight of an object calculated?
4. How much would you weigh on the moon?
5. Why would your weight on the moon be less than that on the earth?
6. Why do the objects on the earth fall to the ground?

前置詞＋関係代名詞

This is *the house*. ← The carpenter built *the house*.（前置詞なし）
→ This is [*the house* **which(that)** the carpenter built].

（これが、[その大工が建てた家] です）

This is the house. ← The carpenter lives **in** *the house*.（前置詞あり）
→ This is [*the house* **in which** the carpenter lives].

（これが、[その大工が住んでいる家] です）

これらの特殊な場合として、先行詞が「場所」や「時」、「原因・理由」、「方法」などをあらわすときに「前置詞＋関係代名詞」と同じ内容を**関係副詞**1語で表すことができます。（→p. viii 関係副詞を参照）

Sapporo is *the city*. ← I was born and brought up in the city.
→ Sapporo is *the city* **in which** I was born and brought up.
→ Sapporo is *the city* **where** I was born and brought up.

名詞を強調するsuch

形容詞としての**such**は名詞（句）を強調する（目立たせる）はたらきを持ちます。名詞（句）が冠詞を伴う場合、一般的な形容詞は冠詞と名詞（句）の間に置かれますが、suchは冠詞の前に置かれることに注意が必要です。

He lives in a large house.（彼は大きな家に住んでいる）
→ I have never seen **such** a large house.
（私はそんな大きな家を見たことがない）

次の例のように、**such＋名詞＋関係詞節**の形で「〜であるような○○を…という」のような**定義文**を作ることができます。

Such a quantity **that** has both magnitude and direction is called a vector.（大きさと方向の両方を持つような量をベクトルという）

「対比」を表すwhile（〜に対し、一方…）

接続詞**while**には、「〜する間」という**同時進行**の意味と、「〜に対し、一方…」「〜であるが」という**対比**の意味があります。後者の場合、主節の後にコンマ（, ）で区切ってwhile節が続きます。

Hydrogen and oxygen are elements, **while** water is a compound of them.（水素と酸素は元素であり、一方、水はそれらの化合物である）

形式主語

名詞的用法の不定詞句やthat節が主語である場合、これらをそのまま主語の位置に置かず、形式主語のitを使って文を作ることが一般的です。たとえば「〜することは…だ」のような文では、It is … to (do). という形になります。

- If the mass of a stationary object is greater, **it** is more difficult **to** move it.（静止した物体の質量が大きい場合、それを動かすことはより難しい）
- **It** is a scientific fact **that** the earth rotates around the sun.
  （地球が太陽の周りを回っているというのは科学的事実だ）

the＋比較級 〜 , the＋比較級 …（〜すればするほど…／〜であればあるほど…）

2つの動作や状態が関連し合って変化することを表します。

The greater the mass of an object is, **the greater** force is needed to change the velocity of it.（物体の質量が大きいほど、その物体の速度を変えるのに大きな力が必要になる）

文脈から意味が明らかな場合、動詞が省略されることがあります。

The greater the resultant force (is), **the greater** the acceleration of the object (is).（合力が大きいほど物体の加速度は大きい）

使役動詞

「〜させる」という意味を持つ動詞を**使役動詞**といいます。使役動詞の**make**, **let**, **have**は［**make / let / have**］＋ **O** ＋ **動詞（原形）**という形で使われるという特徴があります。

それぞれの使役動詞が持つ意味（ニュアンス）は以下の通りです。
　make：（相手の意思にかかわらず／強制的に）「〜させる」
　let：（相手の意思を尊重して／状況を変えないよう）「〜させ（てや）る」
　have：（必要なことを実現するために）「〜させる／してもらう」

- A force is defined as a push or a pull that **makes** an object change in motion.（力とは、物体の運動を変化させるような「押し・引き（する力）」であると定義される）
- A balanced force **lets** a stationary object remain stationary.
  （釣り合った力は、静止した物体を静止したままにさせる）
- The driver **had** the mechanic check the engine.
  （ドライバーは整備士にエンジンをチェックさせた）

仮定法 (2)　(→ p. 18　仮定法 (1) 参照)

文脈から意味が明らかな場合、**従属節 (if節)** を省略して**主節の述語動詞**を **would + 動詞の原形**という形にしたものも仮定法過去の文です。下の例文は、"if you measured your weight on the moon"（もし月面上で体重を計ったら）という従属節が省略されていると考えられます。

Can you imagine how much you **would** weigh on the moon?

一般に**丁寧表現**とされている **would like to ～**も仮定法過去による表現の一つです。

(If you **could** give me something to drink,) I **would** like to have a cup of coffee.

倍数 (分数) 表現　(→ p. 9　倍数表現 参照)

「○**分の**△」のような分数は、「○**倍**」を表す倍数表現と同じように表すことができます。

- The mass of the moon is about **one sixth** that of the earth.
  （月の質量は地球の質量の約 6 分の 1 です）
- He owns **a quarter** the area of the land.
  （彼はその土地の面積の 4 分の 1 を所有している）
- A female Asian elephant weighs about **two thirds** that of a male.
  （メスのアジア象の体重はオスの約 3 分の 2 です）

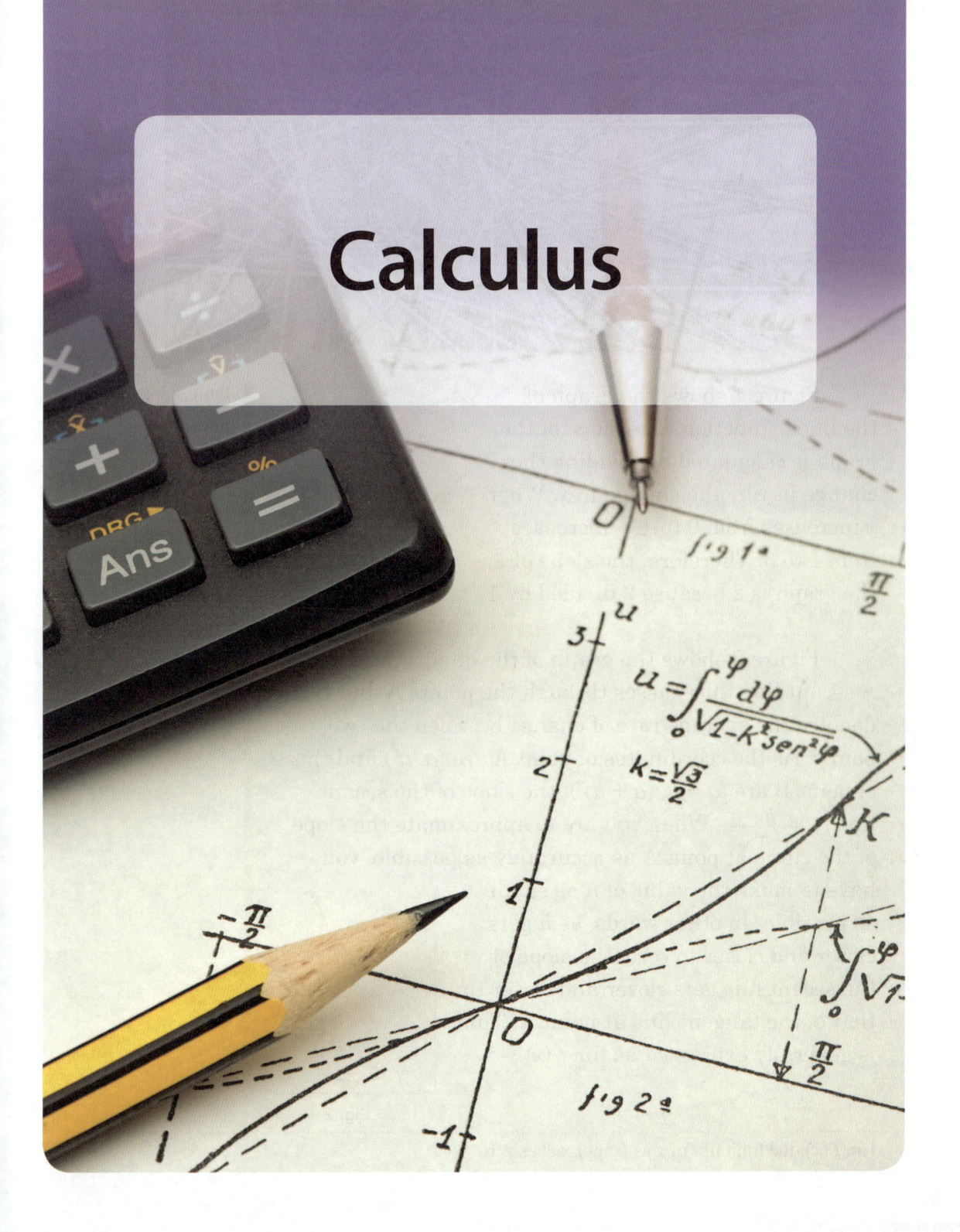

Lesson 4

Calculus

Part 1

Limits

Figure 1 shows the graph of the linear function. The slope of the graph is calculated by dividing the change in y by the change in x. When

5 x increases from 0 to 1, y increases from 1 to 3. Therefore, the slope of the graph is 2 because 2 divided by 1 is 2.

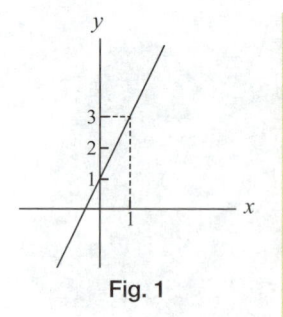

Fig. 1

limit [límit]

linear [líniər]

quadratic [kwɑdrǽtik]

secant [síːkænt]

accurately [ǽkjurətli]

Figure 2 shows the graph of the quadratic function.

10 A secant line that passes through the points A and B denotes the average rate of change between the two points. As the coordinates of point A are (a, a^2) and those of point B are $(a + h, (a + h)^2)$, the slope of the secant line is $\frac{(a+h)^2 - a^2}{h}$. When you are to approximate the slope

15 of the curve at point A as accurately as possible, you have to make the value of h as small as possible. In other words, as h gets closer and closer to zero, the slope of the secant line gets closer and closer to

20 that of the tangent line at point A. This is generally expressed as $\lim\limits_{h \to 0} f(x)$.

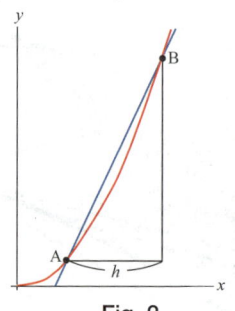

Fig. 2

$\lim\limits_{h \to 0} f(x)$: the limit of f of x as h approaches zero

32

Grammar and Expressions

as ～ as possible（できるだけ～） （→ p. 38）

When you are to approximate the slope of the curve at point A **as** accurately **as possible**, you have to make the value of h **as** small **as possible**.

比較級 and 比較級（だんだん～になる／する） （→ p. 38）

As h gets **closer and closer** to zero, the slope of the secant line gets **closer and closer** to that of the tangent line at point A.

Practice

A 日本語と同じ意味になるように、（　　）内に適切な語を入れましょう。

1. そのグラフはx軸にどんどん近づいていくが、交わることはない。

   The graph gets (　　) (　　) (　　) to the x-axis, but they never cross.

2. 飛行機は離陸直後からどんどんスピードを上げていった。

   The airplane got (　　) (　　) (　　) just after the take-off.

3. 堤防が決壊し、水がどんどんと町に流れてきた。

   The dike broke and (　　) (　　) (　　) (　　) flowed into the town.

4. 彼はできるだけ長く水中にいられるよう、深く息を吸った。

   He took a deep breath to stay under water (　　) (　　) (　　) (　　).

5. かれらは車体をできるだけ軽くするため、鉄板をできるだけ薄くした。

   They made the iron sheet (　　) (　　) (　　) (　　) in order to make the body (　　) (　　) (　　) (　　).

B 日本語と同じ意味になるように、［　　］内の語句を並べ替えて言ってみましょう。

1. この関数では、yの変化量はxの変化量に比例する。

   In this function, [in / in / in / is / the change / proportion / the change / to / x / y].

2. このグラフの傾きは、速度の変化の平均の割合を表している。

   The slope of this graph [average / denotes / in / of / the / rate / the change / velocity].

3. πの値の近似値を求めるために、円周を直径で割りなさい。

   [approximate / of / pi / the / to / value], [by / divide / the circumference / the diameter].

33

Differential Calculus

1-52~55

On the graph of $y = f(x)$, the slope of the tangent line at one point whose coordinates are $(a, f(a))$ can be found by calculating the limit of $\frac{f(a+h) - f(a)}{h}$ as h approaches zero. The function that gives the slope of

5 the graph of a function at an arbitrary point is called the derivative of the function $f(x)$, which is denoted as $f'(x)$. The process of finding a derivative is called differentiation.

An easy way to find the derivative of a function like

10 $f(x) = 2x^3$ is to multiply the coefficient by the exponent, and then decrease the exponent by 1. Hence the derivative of

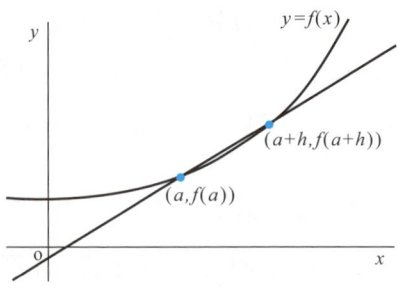

15 $f(x) = 2x^3$, which is denoted as $f'(x)$, is $6x^2$.

A polynomial function like $f(x) = x^3 + 2x^2 + 1$ can be considered the sum of the monomial functions of $g(x) = x^3$, $h(x) = 2x^2$ and $j(x) = 1$. The derivative of

20 the function $f(x)$ is the sum of the derivatives of each function. Therefore, $f'(x) = g'(x) + h'(x) + j'(x)$. Hence $f'(x) = 3x^2 + 4x \; (+ 0)$.

differential
[dìfərénʃəl]

calculus [kǽlkjələs]

derivative
[dirívətiv]

process [prá:ses]

differentiation
[dìfərənʃiéiʃən]

coefficient
[kòuifíʃənt]

exponent
[ikspóunənt]

hence [héns]

polynomial
[pàlinóumiəl]

sum [sʌm]

monomial
[mɑnóumiəl]

prime [práim]

....

f'(x) : *f*-prime of *x*

🔤 Grammar and Expressions

to不定詞 (名詞用法) と動名詞 (→ p. 38)

The process of **finding** a derivative is called differentiation.
An easy way **to find** the derivative of a function is **to multiply** the coefficient by the exponent, and then decrease the exponent by 1.

📝 Practice

A 日本語の意味を考えて、次の (　　) 内のうち正しいものを選びましょう。

1. 私は読書が好きです。

   I like (reading, to read) books.

2. 列車の切符を予約する簡単な方法は、インターネットを使うことだ。

   An easy way of (reserving, to reserve) train tickets is (using, to use) the Internet.

3. ここで写真を撮ったことを覚えていますか。

   Do you remember (taking, to take) pictures here?

4. 実験中はノートを取ることを忘れないように。

   Do not forget (taking, to take) notes during the experiment.

B 日本語と同じ意味になるように、[　　] 内の語句を並べ替えて言ってみましょう。

1. このグラフ上で x 座標が 5 である点における y の値を求めなさい。

   Find [5 / at / is / of / the value / the point / whose / x-coordinate / y] on this graph.

2. このグラフの任意の点における接線の傾きはどうすれば求められますか。

   How [an / at / arbitrary / can / find / point / the slope / of / the tangent line / you] on this graph?

3. $f'(x)$ は、関数 $f(x)$ の導関数を表す。

   [denotes / $f'(x)$ / $f(x)$ / of / the derivative / the function].

4. a の値を 3 倍し、それを b の値で割りなさい。

   [3 / a / by / multiply / of / the value], and [b / by / divide / it / of / the value].

5. その実験の結果は成功であったと考えられる。

   [a / be / can / of / success / the experiment / the result / considered].

Integral Calculus

1-56~60

If the derivative of a function is $2x$, what is it the derivative of?

One of the answers is x^2 because the derivative of x^2 is $2x$. However, the function whose derivative becomes $2x$
5 is not only x^2 but also $x^2 + 1$ or $x^2 + \pi$ and so on, because any constant in a function becomes zero when they are differentiated. So, we say $x^2 + C$ is the antiderivative of $2x$, where C is the unknown constant. The antiderivative of $2x$ is denoted as $\int 2x \, dx$. The antiderivative is also
10 called the indefinite integral.

To find the antiderivative of x^n with respect to x, you have to increment the exponent by 1 and divide it by the same value. This is called the reverse power rule. However, you must not forget to add the constant C. For
15 example, $\int x^3 \, dx$ is going to be $\frac{x^4}{4} + C$.

A definite integral, whose expression resembles an indefinite integral except for having the integral interval like $\int_a^b f(x) \, dx$, denotes the area surrounded by the curve of the function and the lines
20 $x = a$, $x = b$, and x-axis. For example, by calculating $\int_1^2 x^3 \, dx$, you can find the area surrounded by the curve of $y = x^3$ and the lines $x = 1$, $x = 2$
25 and x-axis.

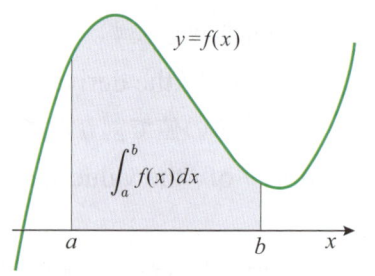

integral [íntəgrəl]

differentiate [dìfərénʃièit]

antiderivative [æ̀ntaidirívətiv]

indefinite [indéfənit]

respect [rispékt]

increment [ínkrəmənt]

reverse [rivə́ːrs]

power [páuər]

definite [défənət]

except [iksépt]

interval [íntərvəl]

surround [səráund]

$\int 2x \, dx$: the integral of $2x \, dx$ **with respect to** $\sim$: $\sim$について（関して）
except for $\sim$: $\sim$を除いて

Grammar and Expressions

前置詞を伴うWH疑問文　(→ p. 39)

If the derivative of a function is $2x$, **what** is it **the derivative of**?

except と except for　(→ p. 39)

The expression of a definite integral resembles an indefinite integral **except for** having the integral interval.

Practice

A　日本語と同じ意味になるように、（　　）内に適切な語を入れましょう。

1. この方程式をxについて解きなさい。

   Solve this equation (　　　) (　　　) (　　　) x.

2. 私以外の全員がピクニックに行きました。

   Everybody (　　　) (　　　) me went to picnic.

3. 何名かの学生を除き、ほぼ全ての学生が今日卒業した。

   (　　　) (　　　) a few students, almost all students graduated today.

4. 二次方程式の一般形は$ax^2 + bx + c = 0$である。ただしaは0ではない。

   The general form of (　　　) (　　　) is $ax^2 + bx + c = 0$, (　　　) a is not 0.

B　日本語と同じ意味になるように、［　　］内の語句を並べ替えて言ってみましょう。

1. 重水素は何の同位体ですか。

   [an / deuterium / is / isotope / of / what]?

2. 関数$y = ax^2 + bx + c$において、aは何の係数ですか。

   In the function $y = ax^2 + bx + c$, [a / coefficient / is / the / of / what]?

3. 豆腐は何からできているのですか。

   [from / is / made / tofu / what]?

4. 水の分子は何の原子からできているのですか。

   [a / atoms / is / made / molecule / of / up / water / what]?

5. この放物線はどんな関数のグラフですか。

   [function / graph / is / of / parabola / the / this / what]?

as ～ as possible（できるだけ～）

同等比較（**as ～ as**）の応用です。

Run **as** fast **as** you can.（できるだけ速く走りなさい）

→ Run **as** fast **as possible**.

When you are to approximate the slope of the curve at point A **as** accurately **as possible**, you have to make the value of h **as** small **as possible**.（点 A における曲線の傾きをできるだけ正確に近似しようとしたら、h の値をできる限り小さくしなければならない）

比較級 and 比較級（だんだん～になる／する）

比較級の形容詞・副詞を重ねることで、その程度の変化を表すことができます。

- The balloon flew **higher and higher**.
（気球はどんどん高く上がっていった）
- As h gets **closer and closer** to zero, the slope of the secant line gets **closer and closer** to that of the tangent line at point A.（h が 0 に近づくにつれて、割線の傾きは点 A における接線の傾きに近づいていく）

to不定詞（名詞用法）と動名詞

動詞を名詞化して「～すること」という意味を表すものには、**to不定詞（名詞用法）**と**動名詞**がありますが、その使い分けには注意が必要です。

to不定詞は、前置詞toが「～へ、～に」という**方向**や**目的**を持つニュアンスがあることからわかるように、主としてこれからすること（未来の行動）や目的を持った行動、あるいはその行動に向かう気持ちを表すのに使います。

- Don't forget **to call** him tonight.
（彼に電話することを忘れないように）◀未来の行動
- One of the easy ways to find the derivative of a function is **to multiply** the coefficient by the exponent, then decrease the exponent by 1.
（関数の導関数を求める簡単な方法の一つは、係数に乗数を掛け、さらに乗数を 1 減らすことである）◀目的のある動作
- I like **to read** books.（本を読みたい）◀その行動に向かう気持ちがある

動名詞は、その行動や動作が一つのまとまった「もの・こと」としてとらえられる場合、あるいはすでに行った過去の行動であることを表すのに使います。

- The process of **finding** a derivative is called differentiation.
  （導関数を求める過程を微分という）　◀一連の動作
- I like **reading** books.（私は読書が好きです）　◀読書という「もの（こと）」
- Don't you remember **visiting** the park with me?
  （僕と一緒にその公園へ行ったことを覚えていないのかい）　◀過去の行動

前置詞を伴うWH疑問文

疑問文としての語順は、通常のWH疑問文と同じです。次の例題を見て、この形の文の作り方を確認しましょう。

例題1：2xは何の導関数ですか。

　Step 1）問いたい部分を疑問詞にして、平叙文の語順で書いてみる。

　　　　　→ $2x$ is the derivative of (what).（$2x$ は○○の導関数である）

　Step 2）疑問文の語順にする（疑問詞を文頭に、助動詞／ be 動詞を主語の前に移動）。

　　　　　→ **What** is $2x$ the derivative of?

例題2：（あなたは）何のためにこの液体を沸騰させるのですか。

　Step 1）You (do) boil this liquid for (what).
　　　　　（あなたは○○のためにこの液体を沸騰させる）

　Step 2）**What** do you boil this liquid for?

except と except for

except (for) + 名詞（句） は「〜を除いて」「〜以外は」という意味ですが、使い方に注意する必要があります。

except (for) で除外された「残り」が、「すべて」または「ゼロ」の概念を表す場合は、**except / except for** どちらも使えます。

- **Everyone** except (for) me went home .（私以外の全員が帰宅した）
- There was **nothing** to eat except (for) a piece of bread.
  （一切れのパン以外、食べるものは何もなかった）

特定の人や物について述べるとき、および **except** で始まる副詞句が文頭に置かれるときは **except for** を使います。

- This computer works perfectly except for the keyboard.
  （このコンピューターは、キーボード以外は完璧に動作します）
- **Except for** the president, nobody knew the fact.
  （社長を除いて、誰もその事実を知らなかった）

前置詞や接続詞の前に置かれる場合は、必ず **except** が単独で使われます。

- I take a walk every morning **except on** a rainy day.
  （私は雨の日以外は毎朝散歩する）
- Never open this box **except when** it is urgent.
  （緊急の場合を除き、この箱を開けるべからず）

Waves

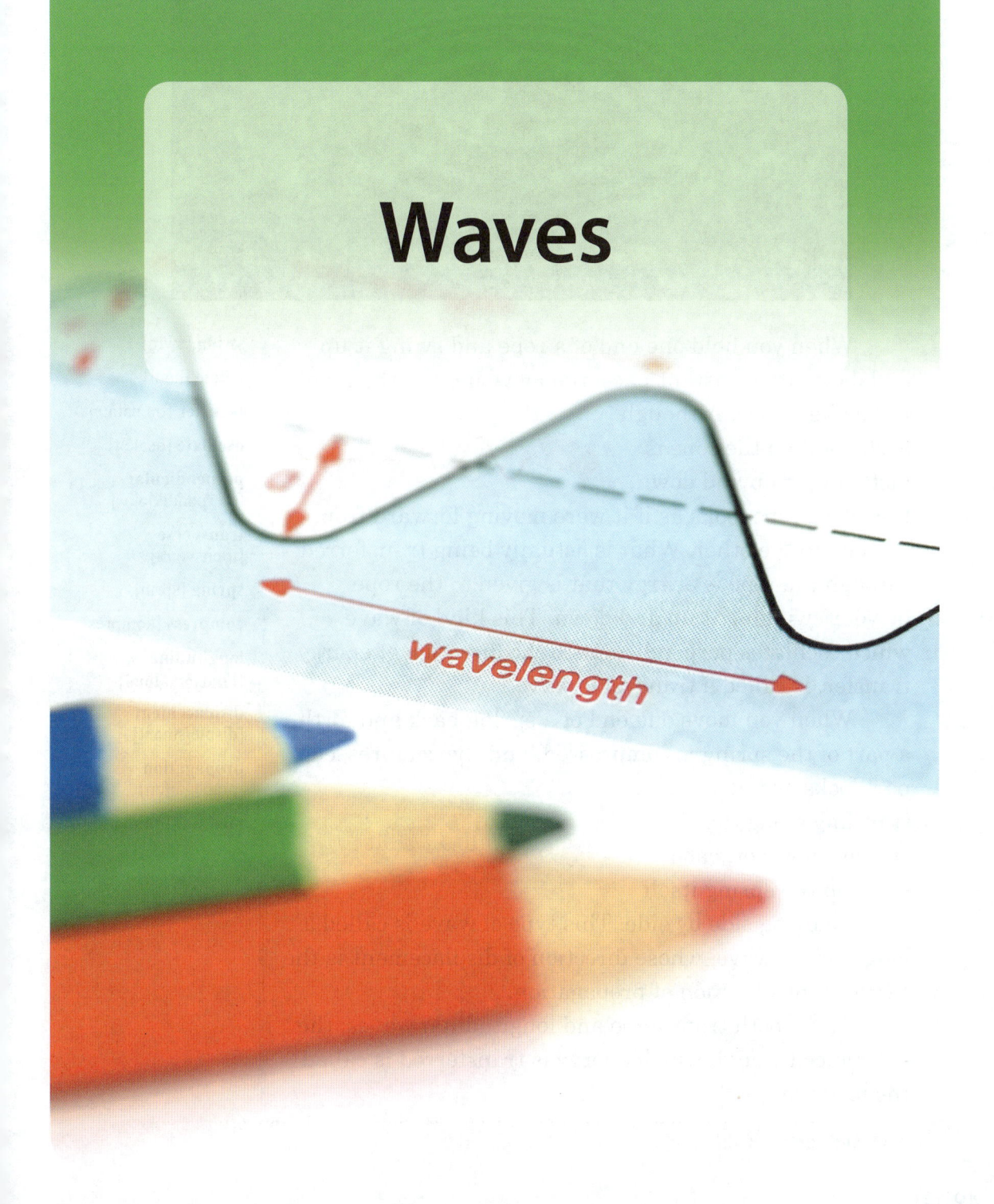

Types of Waves

1-61~64

When you hold one end of a rope and swing it up
and down at a constant pace, the movement of the rope
looks like waves. Although
each point on the rope is
5 just moving up and down,
the whole rope looks as if it were moving forward from
one end to the other. What is actually being transferred
through the rope is energy that is given to the rope
by your swinging it up and down. This kind of wave,
10 which oscillates perpendicular to the direction of energy
transfer, is called a transverse wave.

When you move one end of a spring back and forth,
a part of the spring is compressed, and the compressed
part looks as if it were
15 traveling along the
spring. However, each
point on the spring itself
is just moving side by side. This type of wave is called a
longitudinal wave, whose direction of displacement is the
20 same as the direction of propagation.

As for both transverse and longitudinal waves, the
substance through which energy is transferred is called
the medium.

swing [swíŋ]

whole [hóul]

transfer [trænsfə́:r]

oscillate [ásəlèit]

perpendicular
[pə̀:rpəndíkjələr]

transverse
[trænsvə́:rs]

spring [spríŋ]

compress [kəmprés]

longitudinal
[làndʒətú:dinəl]

displacement
[displéismənt]

propagation
[pràpəgéiʃən]

medium [mí:diəm]

----

back and forth：前後に

ABC Grammar and Expressions

| as if 〜を用いた仮定表現（まるで〜のように）(→ p. 50)

The whole rope looks **as if** it <u>were moving</u> forward from one end to the other.

| 動名詞の意味上の主語 (→ p. 50)

Energy that is given to the rope by **your** <u>swinging</u> it up and down.

| 受動態の進行形 (→ p. 51)

What <u>**is**</u> actually **<u>being transferred</u>** through the rope is energy…

Practice

A 日本語と同じ意味になるように、（　　）内の動詞を正しく書き換えましょう。

1. 私たちはその物理学者がノーベル賞を受賞したことを誇りに思う。

We are proud of the physicist's (have) (win) the Nobel Prize.

2. その理論はまだ検証中です。

The theory (be) still (be) (examine).

3. この部屋はとても蒸し暑い。窓を開けてもいいかい。

It's so hot and humid here in this room. Do you mind my (open) the window?

4. そのロボットはまるで人間のように流暢に話す。

That robot speaks so fluently as if it (be) human.

B 日本語と同じ意味になるように、（　　）内に適切な語を入れましょう。

1. 横波についていえば、ロープ上のそれぞれの点は上下に動いているだけだ。

(　　) (　　) a transverse wave, each point on the rope is just moving
(　　) (　　) (　　).

2. この電線は、大きな電流が流れる回路の一部です。

This wire is a part of the circuit (　　) (　　) a large current flows.

3. 掛け時計の振り子が行ったり来たりしている。

The pendulum of the wall clock is oscillating (　　) (　　) (　　).

4. 優勝したとき、私はまるで夢を見ているような気分でした。

Winning the tournament, I felt (　　) (　　) I (　　) in a dream.

Properties of Waves

1-65~69

When you swing one end of a string up and down just once, a pulse wave will propagate along the string. If you continue swinging the
5 string up and down periodically, a periodic wave will be formed.

The highest and the lowest points where the wave reaches are respectively called the crest and the trough of the wave. The vertical distance from the level point to the
10 crest or the trough is called the amplitude of the wave.

The distance from one crest to the next, which is the same as the distance between two troughs, is called
15 the wavelength. The wavelength is generally denoted by the Greek letter λ (lambda).

The period of the wave is defined as how many seconds it takes for the wave to make one up-and-down cycle. In other words, the inverse of the period represents
20 how many cycles the wave makes in one second. This is called the frequency of the wave, which is measured in hertz (Hz).

string [stríŋ]

pulse [pʌ́ls]

propagate [prɑ́pəgèit]

periodically [pìəriɑ́dikəli]

crest [krést]

vertical [vɔ́:rtikəl]

level [lévl]

trough [trɔ́(:)f]

amplitude [ǽmplitù:d]

wavelength [wéivlèŋkθ]

inverse [ìnvɔ́:rs]

represent [rèprizént]

frequency [frí:kwənsi]

hertz [hɔ́:rts]

Greek letter：ギリシャ文字

Grammar and Expressions

> **to不定詞の意味上の主語** （→ p. 51）
>
> … how many seconds it takes **for** the wave **to** make one up-and-down cycle.

Practice

A 日本語と同じ意味になるように、（　　）内に適切な語を入れましょう。

1. このスーパーコンピューターがその計算を行うのに1秒もかからない。

   It (　　　) less than one second (　　　) this supercomputer (　　　) carry out the calculation.

2. 人口密度は単位面積に住んでいる人の数と定義される。

   The population density (　　　) (　　　) (　　　) the (　　　) of people living in a unit area.

3. 波の周波数は、その波が1秒間に作るサイクルの回数として定義される。

   The frequency of the wave (　　　) (　　　) (　　　) how (　　　) (　　　) the (　　　) (　　　) in one second.

4. かれらがこの問題を議論するには長い時間がかかるかもしれない。

   It may take a long time (　　　) them (　　　) discuss this issue.

5. かれらはその問題について何時間も議論し続けた。

   They (　　　) (　　　) the issue for hours.

B 日本語と同じ意味になるように、［　　］内の語句を並べ替えて言ってみましょう。

1. 卒業するために何単位を取得しなければならないかチェックした方がいい。

   You should check [credits / how / many / must / take / you] to graduate.

2. 無料でインターネットが使えるホテルはありますか。

   Is there a hotel [can / for free / I / the Internet / use / where]?

3. その旅行が実施されるかどうかは、参加を希望する人数によって決まる。

   It depends on [are / going / how / in / it / many / part / people / to / take] if the trip will be carried out or not.

4. アスリートにとって、試合の前に何を食べるべきかを学ぶことは大切だ。

   It is important [athletes / eat / for / learn / to / to / what] before the game.

Doppler Effect

CD
1-70~73

Suppose you are observing a wave whose wavelength and frequency are λ (m) and f (Hz) respectively. This means the wave travels $\lambda \times f$ meters per second, which also means the velocity of the wave
5 v(m/s) can be calculated by multiplying its wavelength and frequency. These relationships are expressed by the formula $v = \lambda \times f$, which can be modified as $\lambda = \frac{v}{f}$ and $f = \frac{v}{\lambda}$.

The speed of sound in the air is generally
10 approximated as 340 m/s. If you hear a sound whose frequency is 440 Hz, you can determine that its wavelength is approximately 0.77 meters by plugging the numbers into the formula above.

Let's think about a case
15 in which the source of sound is approaching toward you at 10 m/s. Although the sound travels at 340 m/s, in this case the sound travels only 330 meters per second because
20 the sound source is moving 10 meters toward you every second. So, the apparent wavelength will be shorter than in the case where the sound source is stationary. This means the pitch of the sound will be higher than it really is. For the same reason, when the sound source
25 is retreating from you, it sounds lower-pitched. This phenomenon is called the Doppler effect.

suppose [səpóuz]

observe [əbzə́:rv]

modify [mάdəfài]

determine [ditə́:rmin]

plug [plʌ́g]

source [sɔ́:rs]

apparent [əpǽrənt]

retreat [ritrí:t]

pitch [pítʃ]

phenomenon [finάmənὰn]

Doppler effect：ドップラー効果

Grammar and Expressions

比較を表す接続詞 than （→ p. 51）

The apparent wavelength will be shorter **than** in the case where the sound source is stationery.

suppose の用法 （→ p. 51）

Suppose you are observing a wave whose wavelength and frequency are λ (m) and f (Hz) respectively.

複合形容詞 （→ p. 52）

When the sound source is retreating from you, it sounds **lower-pitched**.

Practice

A 日本語と同じ意味になるように、（　　）内に適切な語を入れましょう。

1. あなたが今、月にいるとして、そこで体重がどれくらいになるか計算しなさい。

   (　　) you are on the moon and calculate (　　) (　　) you (　　) there.

2. その音は実際よりも高く聞こえるかもしれません。

   You may hear the sound higher (　　) (　　) really (　　).

3. x に0を代入することで y 切片が求められる。

   You can find the y-intercept (　　) (　　) (　　) 0 for x.

4. このスマートフォンは以前より使える時間が短くなった。

   This smartphone works (　　) (　　) before.

5. ドローンの間は3メートルの距離を維持する必要があります。

   (　　) (　　) must be maintained between the drones.

6. 分銅セットは1グラム分銅10個と5グラム分銅5個で販売されています。

   The weight set comes with (　　) (　　) weights and (　　) (　　) weights.

B 日本語と同じ意味になるように、[　　]内の語句を並べ替えて言ってみましょう。

1. 波の速度は波長と周波数を掛けることで計算することができる。

   The velocity of the wave can be calculated [and / by / frequency / its / multiplying / wavelength].

2. オームの法則 V=RI は、I=V/R や R=V/I と書き換えることができる。

   Ohm's law V=RI [and / as / be / can / modified / I=V/R / R=V/I].

Part 4

Light Waves

1-74~78

Although waves generally need a medium to propagate through, only electromagnetic waves can travel through a vacuum. Electromagnetic waves contain radio waves, such as light, x-rays, gamma rays and so on.

5 Electromagnetic waves whose wavelengths are between 390 to 700 nanometers are called visible light, or simply light, because human eyes can respond to them.

The speed of electromagnetic waves, including light, is approximately 3.0×10^8 (300 million) meters per second.

10 Light travels fast enough to go around the earth seven and a half times in one second.

When light travels through a medium such as water, it slows down at a certain rate with respect to the vacuum. The rate, which is called the refractive index,

15 depends on the medium. As the refractive index of water is 1.333, light travels 1.333 times slower than through a vacuum.

The refractive index also depends on the wavelength. When a white light, which is a mixture

20 of all colors of light, goes through a prism, each color refracts separately according to its wavelength. This creates a spectrum, which looks like a rainbow.

electromagnetic [ilèktroumæɡnétik]

vacuum [vǽkjuːm]

radio [réidiou]

x-ray [éksrèi]

nanometer [nǽnəmìːtər]

visible [vízəbl]

respond [rispánd]

refractive [rifrǽktiv]

index [índeks]

depend [dipénd]

mixture [míkstʃər]

refract [rifrǽkt]

spectrum [spéktrəm]

gamma ray：ガンマ線

🔤 Grammar and Expressions

> | **~ enough to (do)** (→ p. 52)
>
> It travels *fast **enough** to **go*** around the earth seven and a half times in one second.

📝 Practice

A 日本語と同じ意味になるように、（　　）内に適切な語を入れましょう。

1. 紫外線は、波長が14ナノメートルから400ナノメートルであるが、皮膚にダメージを与えるといわれている。

Ultraviolet rays, (　　) (　　) are from 14 nm to 400 nm, are said to (　　) our skin.

2. 物質はある温度で液体から気体に変化するが、その温度は沸点といわれる。

Substances change from liquid to gas (　　) a (　　) (　　), (　　) is called the boiling point.

3. 真空中を自由落下する2つの物体は同時に着地する。

Two objects (　　) freely (　　) a (　　) will reach the ground (　　) (　　) (　　) (　　).

B 日本語と同じ意味になるように、［　　］内の語句を並べ替えて言ってみましょう。

1. 波は一般的に（それが）通るための媒体を必要とする。

Waves generally [a medium / need / propagate / through / to].

2. このタブレット型コンピューターはどこへでも持っていけるほど軽い。

This tablet computer is [anywhere / enough / light / take along / to].

3. pH値が6以下の物質は酸性に分類される。

A substance [6 / classified / equal / is / is / less / or / pH / than / to / whose] as acid.

4. 時間に正確であることは、日本人が持っている長所の一つだと思う。

I believe [being / have / is / Japanese people / punctual / of / one / that / the virtues].

as if 〜を用いた仮定表現（まるで〜のように）

as if 〜は「（実際はそうではないのだが）まるで〜のように…」という意味を表すときに使われます。事実ではないことを仮定して述べるので、**as if節**は**仮定法過去**（→ p. 18, p. 30参照）になります。

- He talks **as if** he **knew** everything.
  （彼は何でも知っているかのように話す）◀ 実際には知らない
- She behaves **as if** she **were** a little girl.
  （彼女はまるで少女のように振る舞う）◀ 現実は少女ではない

主節の動詞よりも以前の事柄について仮定表現を用いるときは、as if節は**仮定法過去完了**になります。

She looked **as if** she **had seen** a ghost.
（彼女はまるで幽霊でも見たような様子だった）

動名詞の意味上の主語

動名詞の意味上の主語は、**所有格**を用いて表現します。ただし、文の主語と動名詞の主語が同じ場合は、動名詞の意味上の主語は省略します。

- I am proud of **my son's being** kind to everyone.
  （私は息子が誰にでも親切であることを誇りに思う）
- Do you mind **my opening** the window?
  （窓を開けてもいいですか）◀（open の主語は I）
- Do you mind **opening** the window?
  （窓を開けていただけますか）◀（mind も open も主語は you）

なお、動名詞が他動詞の場合や、前置詞の目的語の位置にある場合は、所有格のかわりに目的格が用いられることもあります。

I am sure of **his(him) winning** the first prize.
（私は彼が優勝することを確信している）

受動態の進行形

受動態の進行形は、受動態の **be + 過去分詞**と、進行形の **be + ...ing** を組み合わせた形、すなわち **be + being + 過去分詞**という形になり「〜されているところだ、〜されている最中だ」という意味になります。

The students are cleaning the room.

→ The room **is being cleaned** by the students.

　（教室は学生によって清掃されているところです）

They are building the bridge.

→ The bridge **is being built**.（その橋は建設中だ）

to不定詞の意味上の主語

to不定詞の意味上の主語は、forを使って表します。

It is impossible **for me to finish** writing this program in a week.

（このプログラムを一週間で書き上げるのは私には不可能だ）

比較を表す接続詞 than

接続詞thanは、本来は文と文をつなぐものですが、比較を表す接続詞thanに導かれる節の中では、文脈から明らかな部分はしばしば省略されるため、下の例のように短くなります。

• My brother runs faster **than** I (run).（兄は私より速く走る）

• Prices are becoming higher **than** (they were) before.

（物価が以前より高くなっている）

本文では、... the apparent wavelength will be shorter **than** (it is) in the case where the sound source is stationary. のようにit isが省略されています。

suppose の用法

supposeを文頭で接続詞的に用いることで「〜と仮定してみなさい、仮定してみよう」の意味になります。

Suppose you are observing a wave whose wavelength and frequency are λ (m) and f (Hz) respectively.

（波長と周波数がそれぞれλメートルとfヘルツの波を観測していると仮定してみましょう）

複合形容詞

2語以上の語をハイフン（-）で結んで1語とし、形容詞として使われるものを**複合形容詞**といいます。複合形容詞は、**形容詞 + 名詞**（long-term）、**名詞 + 名詞**（part-time）、**形容詞 + 過去分詞**（ready-made）、**副詞 + 過去分詞**（well-known）など、いろいろな品詞の組み合わせがあります。

下の例文にある**lower-pitched**は、**形容詞 + 名詞+ed**という組み合わせで、good-hearted man（心根の優しい人）やleft-handed pitcher（左投げの投手）などの例があります。

　　When the sound source is retreating from you, it sounds **lower-pitched**.
　　（音源が遠ざかるときは、音は低く聞こえる）

また、計量数が単位と結びついて名詞を修飾する場合もあり、これは数値と単位をハイフンでつないだものです。この場合、単位を表す名詞は常に**単数形**になることに注意しましょう。

- **three-month-old** baby（生後 3 ヶ月の赤ちゃん）
- **20-liter** tank（20 リットル入りのタンク）

～ enough to (do)

（形容詞・副詞）+ enough to (do)は「～するのに十分…である」という意味を表します。この「十分」は「ある目的のために必要な量（程度）を満たしている」というニュアンスで、必ずしも「たっぷり、あり余っている」ことを表すわけではありません。

- We left home *early* **enough to** be in time for the train.
  （私たちは列車に間に合うように早く出かけた）
- Light travels *fast* **enough to** go around the earth seven and a half times in one second.
  （光は一秒間に地球を 7 周半できるほど速く進む）

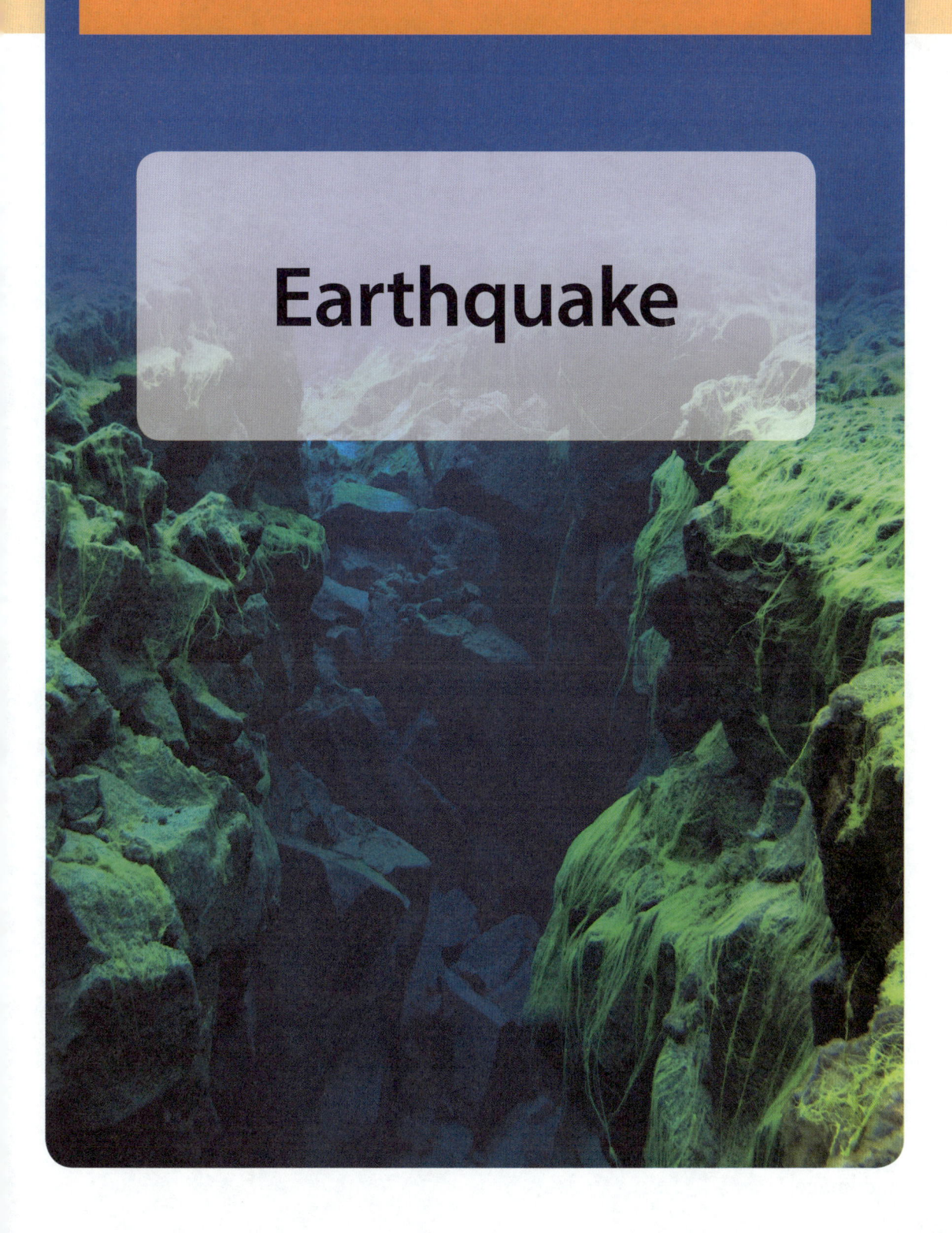

Earthquake

Measurement of Earthquakes

2-01~05

Japan has experienced frequent earthquakes throughout its history.

Just after an earthquake occurs, earthquake information is provided to the public. The information
5 includes the epicenter location, the depth of the focus, the seismic scale, and the distribution of observed seismic intensity. If a tsunami is predicted, a tsunami warning is issued as well.

Seismic intensity scales vary from country to
10 country. In Japan, it is described in the unit of *shindo*. It runs from 0 to 7 with 7 being the strongest. The *shindo* measure varies from place to place, depending on various factors, such as underground conditions, distance from the epicenter, and seismic scale. The seismic scale
15 describes the size of the earthquake, which is usually denoted in a magnitude number.

These factors can also affect the amount of damage caused by the earthquake. However, the largest earthquakes are not always the most disastrous. Even if
20 the magnitude of the earthquake is strong, the further you are from its focus or epicenter, the less shaking you will feel. If you were directly above the focus of the earthquake, the area you are in might suffer catastrophic damage.

experience [ikspíəriəns]

frequent [frí:kwənt]

epicenter [épəsèntər]

location [loukéiʃən]

focus [fóukəs]

seismic [sáizmik]

distribution [dìstribjú:ʃən]

intensity [inténsəti]

predict [pridíkt]

warning [wɔ́:rniŋ]

issue [íʃu:]

vary [vέəri]

affect [əfékt]

disastrous [dizǽstrəs]

further [fə́:rðər]

shake [ʃéik]

suffer [sʌ́fər]

catastrophic [kæ̀təstráfik]

⊞ Grammar and Expressions

～ as well (→ p. 62)

If a tsunami is predicted, a tsunami warning is issued **as well**.

付帯状況 with A …ing ～ (→ p. 62)

It runs from 0 to 7 **with 7 being** the strongest.

部分否定 not always ～ (→ p. 62)

The largest earthquakes are **not always** the most disastrous.

📋 Practice

A 日本語と同じ意味になるように、（　　）内に適切な語を入れましょう。

1. その地震が発生した直後に、地震情報が発表された。

   (　　　) (　　　　) the earthquake occurred, earthquake information was

   (　　　) to the public.

2. その情報で私たちは、震源地の位置や震源の深さ、地震の規模などを知った。

   The information let us know the (　　　) (　　　), the (　　　) of the

   (　　　), and the (　　　) (　　　) of the earthquake.

3. 高価な贈り物が必ずしも子供を喜ばせるとは限らない。

   Expensive gifts (　　　) (　　　) (　　　) make children happy.

4. その有名なスケート選手は、自転車競技にも参加する。

   The famous skater takes part in cycling races (　　　) (　　　).

5. 同じ国の中でも、場所によって挨拶（のしかた）が異なることはよくある。

   Greetings often vary (　　　) (　　　) (　　　) (　　　) even in the same

   country.

B 日本語と同じ意味になるように、[　　　]内の語句を並べ替えて言ってみましょう。

1. シャツのサイズは文字で表され、XLがいちばん大きい。

   Shirt sizes are letter-coded, [being / largest / the / with / XL].

2. 私は、宇宙の大きさについて考えれば考えるほど、わからなくなる。

   [about / I / more / the / think] the size of the universe, [am / I / less /

   sure / the].

Part 2

P-waves and S-waves

2-06~11

Earthquakes produce shockwaves called seismic waves. There are two types of seismic waves, which vary depending on how they travel through the earth.

The faster ones are longitudinal waves called
5 primary waves, or P-waves for short. P-waves propagate as fast as 5 to 7 kilometers per second through solid rock.

The tremors that follow the P-waves are secondary waves, or S-waves for short. They are transverse waves, whose velocity ranges from 3 to 4 kilometers per second
10 depending on the material through which they travel. S-waves propagate only through solid materials while P-waves propagate through either solid, liquid or gas.

When an earthquake occurs, we first feel weak shakes followed by a strong shake. The first small shakes
15 are called preliminary tremors, which are caused by the P-waves. The strong shakes are called the principal shock, which are caused by S-waves.

In a series of earthquakes, the largest one is termed the main shock. Earthquakes that follow the main shock
20 are called aftershocks. Smaller earthquakes that precede the main shock are called foreshocks.

shockwave [ʃákwèiv]

primary [práimèri]

tremor [trémər]

secondary [sékəndèri]

range [réindʒ]

preliminary [prilímənèri]

principal [prínsəpəl]

term [tə́:rm]

aftershock [ǽftərʃàk]

precede [prisí:d]

foreshock [fɔ́:rʃàk]

P-wave：P波　**S-wave**：S波　**preliminary tremor**：初期微動　**principal shock**：主要動

🄰🄱🄲 Grammar and Expressions

as 〜 as + [数値] (→ p. 63)

P-waves propagate **as** fast **as** 5 to 7 kilometers per second through solid rock.

range from A to B (→ p. 63)

… whose velocity **ranges** from 3 to 4 kilometers per second …

📝 Practice

🄰 日本語と同じ意味になるように、(　　) 内に適切な語を入れましょう。

1. 地震は地震波とよばれる衝撃波を発生させる。

   Earthquakes produce (　　　) called (　　　) (　　　).

2. P波は縦波で、秒速5キロから7キロもの速度で伝わる。

   P-waves are (　　　) waves, (　　　) propagate (　　　) (　　　) (　　　) 5 to 7 kilometers per second.

3. S波は横波で、その速度は秒速3キロから4キロまで幅がある。

   S-waves are (　　　) waves, (　　　) velocity (　　　) (　　　) 3 (　　　) 4 kilometers per second.

4. 火災が発生し、大爆発が続いた。

   There occurred a fire (　　　) (　　　) a big explosion.

🄱 日本語と同じ意味になるように、[　　] 内の語句を並べ替えて言ってみましょう。

1. 無数の小規模な地震の後に、火山が噴火した。

   Numerous small earthquakes [of / preceded / the eruption / the volcano].

2. 光の屈折率はその波長によって変化する。

   The refractive index [depending / its / light / of / on / varies / wavelength].

3. 地震波には2種類あるが、それらは地中をどのように伝わるかが異なる。

   There are two types of seismic waves, [are / different / how / in / which / they / through / travel / the earth].

4. 連続する地震の中で最大のものは本震と呼ばれる。

   In a series of earthquakes, [is / largest / one / the main shock / termed / the].

Earthquake Information

CD
2-12~15

When an earthquake occurs, the distance from the epicenter can be determined by the time lag between the arrival of the P- and S-waves. This time lag is proportional to the distance from the epicenter.

5　　Thousands of seismometers have been installed in many locations all over Japan. When an earthquake occurs somewhere in or around Japan, the Japan Meteorological Agency analyzes the data from the seismometers near the focus in order to issue an alert

10 called the earthquake early warning. This warning lets us know the possibility of strong tremors caused by the secondary wave. However, if you are very close to the epicenter, the strong tremors will arrive before the warning. So, if you are inside of a building and feel a

15 strong earthquake, you should immediately get under a table or desk to protect yourself from falling objects.

It is very important to stay informed during any emergency situation. In addition, we have to learn in advance about the underground conditions of the site we

20 live in. We already know how destructive an earthquake can be when it has a shallow inland focus and occurs along an active fault.

lag [lǽg]
arrival [əráivəl]
seismometer [saizmάmətər]
install [instɔ́:l]
meteorological [mì:tiərəládʒikəl]
agency [éidʒənsi]
analyze [ǽnəlàiz]
alert [əlɔ́:rt]
possibility [pὰsəbíləti]
informed [infɔ́:rmd]
emergency [imɔ́:rdʒənsi]
site [sáit]
advance [ədvǽns]
destructive [distrʌ́ktiv]
shallow [ʃǽlou]
fault [fɔ́:lt]

Japan Meteorological Agency：気象庁　　**earthquake early warning**：緊急地震速報
in advance：あらかじめ

🄰🄱🄲 Grammar and Expressions

> **受動態の現在完了形** (→ p. 63)
>
> Thousands of seismometers **have been installed** in many locations all over Japan.
>
> **in or around …** (→ p. 64)
>
> When an earthquake occurs somewhere **in or around** Japan, …

📝 Practice

🄰 日本語と同じ意味になるように、（　）内に適切な語を入れましょう。

1. 最近、私たちの学校にエアコンが設置されました。

Air conditioners (　　　) (　　　) (　　　) in our school recently.

2. 初期微動の時間は震源地からの距離に比例する。

The duration of preliminary tremors (　　　) (　　　) (　　　) the distance from the epicenter.

3. どのような非常事態でも常に情報を得ていることがとても重要だ。

It is very important to (　　　) (　　　) during any emergency situation.

4. その電子顕微鏡を使うには事前に許可を得なければなりません。

You must get permission to use the electron microscope (　　　) (　　　).

5. 何か質問がございましたらお知らせください。

Please (　　　) (　　　) (　　　) if you have any questions.

🄱 日本語と同じ意味になるように、〔　〕内の語句を並べ替えて言ってみましょう。

1. この駅の構内と周辺にはコンビニはありません。

[are / around / convenience stores / in / no / or / there / this station].

2. 気象台は県内に大雪警報を発令した。

[a / an alert / for / heavy / issued / snowfall / the observatory] in the prefecture.

🄲 本文を参考にしながら、日本語と同じ意味の英文を作りましょう。

1. モチベーションを保ち続けることは容易ではありません。

2. 地球温暖化の問題は長いあいだ議論されている。

The Ring of Fire

2-16~20

The earth has a layered structure, including the core, mantle, and crust. The crust, which is the closest to the earth's surface, is not a single solid shell but rather
5 broken up into huge, thick plates called tectonic plates.

So, what is it that makes Japan so seismically active?

Japan is located along the Pacific Ring of Fire.
10 According to scientists, the Ring of Fire includes about 75 percent of the world's active volcanoes and is also responsible for 90 percent of the world's earthquakes. This is because the Ring is the location of most of the earth's subduction zones, where one plate bends and
15 slides underneath the other, curving down into the mantle. Around the Japanese archipelago, the plates on the Pacific side are sinking under the plates on the continental side. This causes the plate on the continental side to warp.
20 When the warping reaches its limit, the plate breaks and rebounds to produce faults and cause earthquakes.

Although major faults mainly form at the plate boundaries between tectonic plates, earthquakes occur
25 not only at the boundaries but also inside the plates.

the Pacific Ring of Fire：環太平洋火山帯

layer [léiər]

structure [strʌ́ktʃər]

mantle [mǽntl]

crust [krʌ́st]

shell [ʃél]

thick [θík]

tectonic [tektánik]

locate [lóukeit]

volcano [vɑlkéinou]

responsible [rispánsəbl]

subduction [səbdʌ́kʃən]

zone [zóun]

underneath [ʌ̀ndərníːθ]

bend [bénd]

archipelago [àːrkəpéləgòu]

warp [wɔ́ːrp]

rebound [ribáund]

boundary [báundəri]

Grammar and Expressions

強調構文 it is A that 〜 (→ p. 64)

What **is it that** makes Japan so seismically active?

Practice

A 日本語と同じ意味になるように、（　　）内に適切な語を入れましょう。

1. 地球は多層構造を持ち、それにはコアやマントル、そして地殻が含まれる。
   The earth has a (　　　) (　　　), (　　　) the core, mantle, and crust.

2. 環太平洋火山帯では世界中の地震の90パーセントが起きている。
   The Pacific Ring of Fire (　　　) (　　　) (　　　) 90 percent of the world's earthquakes.

3. 地球上のすべてのものをその中心方向に引っ張るのが地球の重力である。
   (　　　) (　　　) the earth's gravity (　　　) pulls everything on the earth to the center of it.

4. 電磁ノイズはしばしば装置の異常動作を引き起こす。
   Electro-magnetic noise often (　　　) the device (　　　) operate incorrectly.

B 日本語と同じ意味になるように、[　　]内の語句を並べ替えて言ってみましょう。

1. ゆがみが限界に達すると、プレートは割れたりはね返ったりして、亀裂を生む。
   When the warping reaches its limit, [and / breaks / faults / produce / rebounds / the plate / to].

2. 消化システムの最終段階は大腸で、そこでは食物の水分が吸収される。
   The last part of the digestive system is the large intestine, [absorbed / from / is / the food / water / where].

3. 地球の大気層にはオゾン層があり、そこでは紫外線が吸収される。
   The earth's atmospheric layer has the ozone layer, [absorbed / are / rays / the / ultraviolet / where].

4. 定規を頭でこすると髪が定規にくっつく。これは静電気が引き起こされているるからだ。
   [a plastic ruler / head / on / rub / you / your / when], your hair sticks to the ruler. [a / because / been / created / electricity / has / is / static / this].

～ as well

as wellは主に文末に置かれて「～もまた、そのうえに」と補足的に説明を追加します。

> This computer works very fast, and is very light **as well**.
> （このコンピューターは動作が速く、しかもとても軽い）

似た表現に **A as well as B**（Bだけでなく Aも）があり、同じような意味を表すことができますが、その使い方に注意しましょう。

> He is good at math **as well as** physics.
> （彼は物理だけでなく数学も得意だ）

付帯状況 with A …ing ～

前置詞withは、その前に述べられた物やできごとに何かを付加するはたらきがあります。**with A …ing ～**は「Aが…している状態で～」という**付帯状況**を表します。これは**独立分詞構文**（→p. 10）の一つと考えることができます。

① She was singing **with tears running** down her cheeks.
　（彼女は頬に涙を流しながら歌っていた）
② It runs from 0 to 7 **with 7 being** the strongest.
　（それは 0 から 7 まであり、7 が一番強い）

上の例②のように動詞がbe動詞で、その後に形容詞や分詞が続く場合はbeingが省略され、一般的に**with A +**［形容詞 / 分詞］という形で使われます。

> • Don't speak **with your mouth** (being) **full**.
> 　（口に食べ物をいっぱい入れたまま話してはいけない）
> • He was sitting on the bench **with his legs** (being) **crossed**.
> 　（彼は足を組んでベンチに座っていた）

部分否定 not always ～

not always ～は「常に～とは限らない、必ずしも～というわけではない」という**部分否定**を表します。完全否定との違いをよく理解しましょう。

> • What he says is **not always** right.
> 　（彼が言うことが常に正しいとは限らない）◀ not は always にかかっている。
> • What he says is **not right** at all.
> 　（彼が言うことはまったく間違っている）◀ not は right にかかっている。
> • The largest earthquakes are **not always** the most disastrous.
> 　（最大規模の地震が最も大きな被害をもたらすとは限らない）

部分否定にはこの他にも「**not all**：全てが～というわけではない」「**not necessarily**：必ずしも～というわけではない」や「**not completely**：完全に～というわけではない」、「**not every**：どれもがみな～というわけではない」などの表現があります。

---

as ～ as + [数値]

as A as B は、Bに「数値」をともなう表現が用いられると「BほどもAだ」という強調の意味を持ちます。

- He has **as many as** two thousand CDs.
  （彼は 2,000 枚もの CD を持っている）
- The freshmen visit the library **as often as** five times a week on average.（新入生は平均して週 5 回も図書館に行っている）
- P-waves propagate **as fast as** at 5 to 7 kilometers per second in solid rock.（P 波は岩盤中を秒速 5 ～ 7km もの速さで伝わる）

---

range from A to B

動詞の **range** は、**range from A to B** の形で「（数値）がAからBの範囲に及ぶ」ことを表します。

This school's students **range** from 15 to 20 in age.
（この学校の学生は 15 歳から 20 歳までの年齢幅がある）

受動態の現在完了形

受動態の現在完了形は、完了形の **have + 過去分詞** と受動態の **be + 過去分詞** を組み合わせた形、すなわち **have + been + 過去分詞** の形をとります。意味は、現在完了形のもつ「過去から現在に至るまでの経験、継続、完了・結果」に「受動態」の意味が加わり、過去から現在に至るまでに「～されたことがある」「ずっと～され続けている」「～されている」のようになります。

- I **have been invited** to their house many times.
  （かれらの家には何度も招待されたことがあります）
- Identities of the answerers **have been kept** confidential.
  （回答者の身元は秘密にされています）
- Thousands of seismometers **have been installed** in many locations all over Japan.（数千台の地震計が日本中の様々な場所に設置されている）

in or around …

2つの前置詞をand, orを使って組み合わせることで、前置詞句の意味を広げることができます。たとえばこの **in or around** ならば、「（～の）中または周り」＝「～の周辺」という範囲を示します。

This castle is said to have been built **in or around** 1630.
（この城は 1630 年頃に建てられたといわれている）

or ではなく **and** を使えば、その両方という意味を表します。

Earthquakes often occur **in and around** Japan.
（地震は日本国内やその周辺で頻繁に起こる）

強調構文 It is A that ～

文の要素を強調する方法はいくつかありますが、**It is A that ～** は文の動詞以外の要素を強調するときに使われます。強調したい要素をAの位置に置くことで「**～なのはAだ**」という意味をもつ強調構文になります。

- **It is** architecture **that** I want to major in.（私が専攻したいのは建築学だ）
- **It was** when we were university students **that** we met for the first time.（僕たちが初めて会ったのは大学生の時だった）

この強調構文 **It is A that ～**（**～なのはAだ**）は、特にAが名詞の場合、形式主語構文の **It is A that ～**（**～はAだ**）と混同しがちですが、強調構文は元の文のある要素を **it is** と **that** で挟んでいるわけですから、強調構文からその **it is** と **that** を取り除いてしまえば、元の文に戻ります。

It is at the entrance of this building **that** we promised to meet.
（私たちが会う約束をしたのは、この建物の入り口です）

→ At the entrance of this building, we promised to meet.
（この建物の入り口で、私たちは会う約束をした）

一方、形式主語構文 **It is A that ～** は、**It is** と **that** を取ってしまうと、英文が成立しません。

It is true **that** I made a mistake in my calculations.
（私が計算間違いをしたというのは本当です）

→ __ True __ I made a mistake in my calculations. ◀ 文が成立しない

なお、平叙文で動詞を強調する方法としては、do/does/didを使います。これは、通常は見えない助動詞を可視化することによる強調効果だと言えます。

I love music. → I **do** love music.（音楽が大好きです）

Electromagnetism

Part 1 Magnetic Field

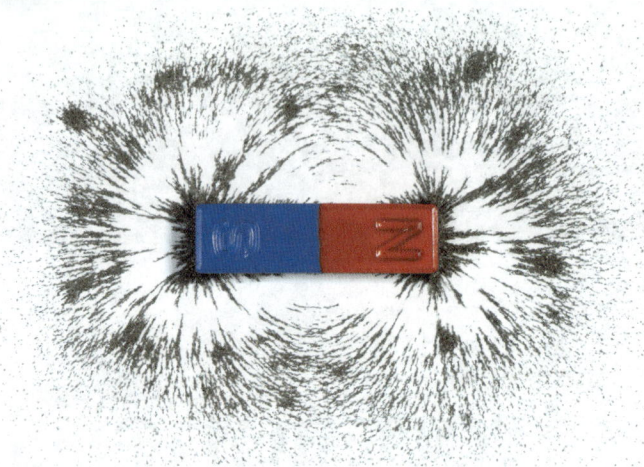

A magnet is a material or an object that generates a magnetic field around it. Every magnet has an N pole and an S pole. Even if you break a magnet into two or more parts, each part is still a magnet with both N and S
5 poles. A set of N and S poles is called a magnetic dipole.

A magnetic field is defined as the area that exerts a force on other magnetic dipoles or electric charges. It is often indicated graphically by means of arrowed lines that run out of the N pole into the S pole as in Figure 1.
10 Each line describes the direction of the magnetic force, and the density of the lines symbolizes the magnetic flux density,
15 which is a vector quantity.

Fig. 1

When an electric current flows through a wire, a magnetic field is generated around the wire. Suppose an electric current flows from right to left in Figure 2. If you grip the wire with your right hand so that your thumb
20 points in the direction of the current flow, your fingers will curl in the same direction of the magnetic field around the wire. This is called the right-hand rule.

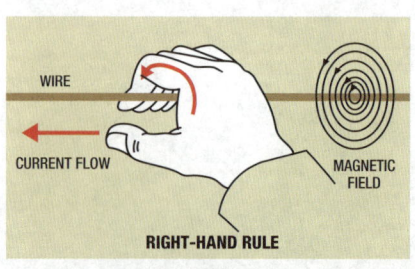

Fig. 2

magnetic [mægnétik]

field [fíːld]

pole [póul]

dipole [dáipòul]

indicate [índikèit]

graphically [grǽfikəli]

arrowed [ǽroud]

density [dénsəti]

flux [flʌ́ks]

grip [gríp]

thumb [θʌ́m]

curl [kə́ːrl]

🅰🅱🅲 Grammar and Expressions

| by means of ～（～を用いて／～によって） (→ p. 72)

It is often indicated graphically **by means of** arrowed lines …

| every と each (→ p. 72)

Every magnet has an N pole and an S pole.
Even if you break a magnet into two or more parts, **each** part is still a magnet with both N and S poles.

📄 Practice

🅐 日本語と同じ意味になるように、（　　）内に適切な語を入れましょう。

1. 塩分濃度が3パーセントになるように水に塩を加えなさい。

   Add salt in the water (　　　) (　　　) its salt concentration reaches 3%.

2. 学生たちは図表を使って発表を行った。

   The students made presentations (　　　) (　　　) (　　　) many diagrams.

3. 科学者たちは実験結果を一つひとつ精査した。

   The scientists examined (　　　) experimental result.

4. 科学者たちは実験結果をすべて精査した。

   The scientists examined (　　　) experimental result.

🅑 日本語と同じ意味になるように、[　　]内の語句を並べ替えて言ってみましょう。

1. どの国にもそれぞれ固有の文化や習慣がある。

   Every country [and / culture / customs / its / has / own].

2. 警官は手話を使ってその少女とやりとりしようとした。

   The policeman [by / communicate / means / of / sign language / the girl / to / tried / with].

3. 要点を理解しやすいように例を挙げましょう。

   I will show you some examples [can / grasp / key points / so / the / that / you] easily.

Part 2

Electromagnetic Force

2-25~27

   Magnetism and electricity are deeply correlated with each other. When an electric current flows through a wire, it generates a magnetic field

5 concentrically around the wire. If the wire is turned into a loop, the magnetic flux is concentrated in the center of the loop. Furthermore, if you wind the wire and make a length of coil called

10 a solenoid, the magnetic flux is much more concentrated, like that of a bar magnet. The magnetic flux density within a solenoid is proportional to the density of turns and the current flowing

15 through it. By putting an iron core through the solenoid, you can make it an electromagnet.

   When an external magnetic field is applied across the wire

20 through which current is flowing, the wire experiences a force. This is the electromagnetic force. You can know the direction of the force using Fleming's left-hand rule. This force is also called the Lorentz force, but the Lorentz force is

25 more exactly defined as the force that a moving charged particle experiences in an electromagnetic field.

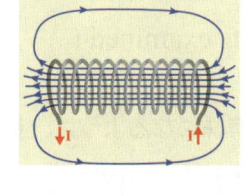

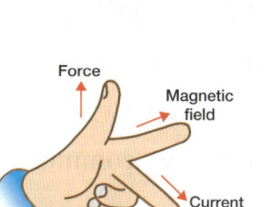

magnetism [mǽgnətìzm]

correlated [kɔ́(:)rəlèitid]

concentrically [kənséntrikəli]

loop [lúːp]

concentrate [kánsəntrèit]

wind [wáind]

solenoid [sóulənɔ̀id]

within [wiðín]

electromagnet [ilèktroumǽgnit]

external [ikstɔ́ːrnəl]

apply [əplái]

Fleming's left-hand rule：フレミングの左手の法則　**the Lorentz force**：ローレンツ力

Grammar and Expressions

experience a force（力を受ける）（→ p. 73）

When an external magnetic field is applied across the wire, the wire **experiences** a force.

範囲を表す within （→ p. 73）

The magnetic flux density **within** a solenoid is proportional to the density of turns.

Practice

A 日本語と同じ意味になるように、（　　）内に適切な語を入れましょう。

1. 磁気と電気は互いに影響を及ぼし合う。

Magnetism and electricity (　　　) each other.

2. 電流は電線のまわりに同心円状に磁場を生じさせる。

An electric current (　　　) a magnetic field (　　　) around the wire.

3. 世界中の関心がその首脳会談（サミット）に集中した。

Global attention (　　　) (　　　) (　　　) the summit.

4. 銅の原子量は鉄のそれよりも大きい。

The atomic mass of copper is larger (　　　) (　　　) (　　　) iron.

5. 食道は口と胃をつなぐ一本の管である。

A gullet is a (　　　) (　　　) tube connecting the mouth to the stomach.

6. より重い物はより大きな重力を受ける。

Heavier things (　　　) more (　　　).

7. ローレンツ力は電荷と磁束密度に比例する。

The Lorentz force is (　　　) (　　　) the electrical charge and the (　　　) (　　　) (　　　).

B 日本語と同じ意味になるように、［　　］内の語句を並べ替えて言ってみましょう。

1. 人口統計では、65歳以上の人を高齢者と定義している。

In demographic statistics, [65 or over / aged / are / are / as / defined / those / who] elderly persons.

2. その実験では、コンクリート柱に大きな力がかかります。

In the experiment, [a / applied / be / force / great / to / will] the concrete column.

Part 3

Electromagnetic Induction

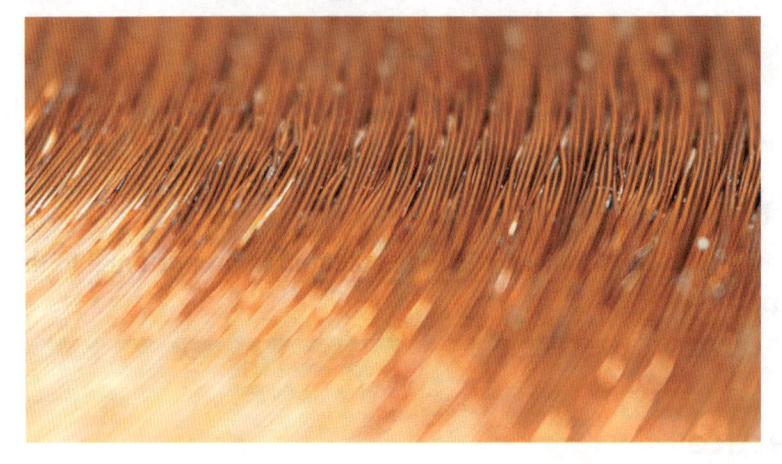

induction
[indʌkʃən]

nor [nɔːr]

induce [indúːs]

oppose [əpóuz]

Here is a loop made with a conducting wire. There is no magnetic field around it, nor is any electric current flowing through it. When you hold a bar

5　magnet and move it toward the loop, current flows through the wire. However, while you are holding the magnet still, no current flows through it. Then, when you start moving the magnet away from the loop, current flows again. Such a phenomenon in which

10　electricity is produced, or induced, by the change of magnetic flux is called electromagnetic induction.

The current produced by electromagnetic induction is called induced current. Once current flows through the conductor, it also produces magnetic flux around the loop.

15　The direction of this flux is always opposite to that of the external magnetic field that has caused the induction. In other words, the direction of induced current is such that it opposes the change of magnetic flux that causes it. This is called Lenz's law.

20　When the magnetic flux around a coil changes, the magnitude of the induced current is proportional to the rate of change in the magnetic flux and the number of turns the coil is wound. This is Faraday's law of induction.

Lenz's law：レンツの法則　**Faraday's law of induction**：ファラデーの電磁誘導の法則

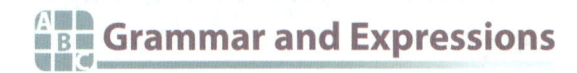

Grammar and Expressions

> **nor + V + S（倒置）：Sもまた〜ない** （→ p. 74）
>
> There is no magnetic field around it, **nor** is any electric current flowing through it.
>
> **Once 〜：いったん〜すると** （→ p. 74）
>
> **Once** current flows through the conductor, it also produces magnetic flux around the loop.
>
> **such that 〜：〜というようなもの** （→ p. 74）
>
> The direction of induced current is **such that** it opposes the change of magnetic flux that causes it.

Practice

A 日本語と同じ意味になるように、（　　）内に適切な語を入れましょう。

1. いったんネット上にメッセージを書き込んだら、それを削除することはほとんど不可能だ。

   (　　　) you put a message on the net, you can (　　　) delete it.

2. 私はその数学の問題を解くことができなかったが、クラスメートのほとんども解けなかった。

   I couldn't solve the math problem, (　　　) (　　　) most of my classmates.

3. この会議は、我々の問題を真正面から扱うようなものであるべきだ。

   This conference should be (　　　) (　　　) it deals with our problems forthright.

B 日本語と同じ意味になるように、[　　]内の語句を並べ替えて言ってみましょう。

1. その物質は私たちの健康に深刻な被害をもたらすようなものだった。

   The substance was [causes / damage / it / such / serious / that] to our health.

2. 運動とは反対の方向に力がかけられると、速度は減少する。

   When [a force / applied / is / motion / of / opposite / to / the direction], the velocity decreases.

by means of ～（～を用いて／～によって）

手段・方法を表します。by, with等の前置詞だけを使って表す場合に比べて、より明示的になります。

- We conducted a survey **by means of** the Internet.
  （我々はインターネットを用いてアンケートを実施した）
- It is often indicated graphically **by means of** arrowed lines.
  （それはしばしば矢印付きの線を使って図示される）

また、この **means**（手段）は、**by any means**（何とかして、どうにかして）や **by no means**（決して～ない）などの形でも用いられます。

- The programmer tried to find the bug **by any means**.
  （そのプログラマーは何とかしてバグを見つけようとした）
- This problem is **by no means** impossible to solve.
  （この問題は決して解決不可能ではない）

every と each

every と **each** はどちらも**複数の要素で構成される集合**について述べるときに用いられ、いずれも**単数扱い**になることが特徴ですが、その用法には次のような違いがあります。

every：それぞれの要素を意識しながら、全体を指す
each：それらの要素の一つひとつを指す

- **Every** student of the class is present today.
  （今日はクラスの全員が出席している）◀クラス全体を意識
- **Each** student of the class is present today.
  （今日はクラスのどの学生も出席している）◀学生一人ひとりを意識
- **Every** one of these babies is just one month old, but **each** has already been displaying a unique personality.
  （ここにいる赤ちゃんはみんなまだ生後1ヶ月だが、すでにそれぞれ独特の個性を見せている）

experience a force（力を受ける）

動詞experienceは、一般的には「経験する」という意味で用いられますが、工学系の文章ではforceやresistanceなどを目的語として「**（力や抵抗などを）受ける**」という意味で用いられることがよくあります。

- A streamlined body **experiences** much less air resistance.
  （流線形の車体は、受ける空気抵抗がずっと少ない）
- Electrically charged particles **experience** a force in the magnetic field.
  （帯電した粒子は磁界中で力を受ける）

範囲を表すwithin

前置詞**within**は、時間について使う場合と、場所について使う場合があり、どちらも「**範囲**」をイメージするとわかりやすいでしょう。時間について言う場合は、下の例のように「**〜以内に**」という意味になります。用法がよく似た前置詞**in**との違いに注意しましょう。

- He will come back **within** five minutes.
  （彼は5分以内に戻ってくる）◀5分かからないかもしれない
- He will come back **in** five minutes.
  （彼は5分で戻ってくる）◀戻ってくるまでに5分かかる

場所について言う場合は、「**〜の中（内側）に**」という意味で、ある範囲の中を指します。この場合、inとの違いはあまり明確ではないのですが、大まかに言えば、inは境界線がはっきりしている場合、withinはそうでない場合に使われることが多いようです。

- There are two convenience stores **within** walking distance.
  （歩いて行ける範囲内にコンビニが2軒あります）
- There are no convenience stores **in** this town.
  （この町にはコンビニがありません）
- The magnetic flux density **within** a solenoid is greater than on the outside.
  （ソレノイド中の磁束密度は外側より大きい）◀ソレノイドは両端が閉じていないので、中と外の境界がはっきりしない

73

nor + V + S（倒置）：Sもまた〜ない

norは否定の繰り返しに用いられる接続詞で「**Sもまた〜ない**」という意味を持ちますが、**norに続く文は主語と動詞が倒置する**という特徴があります。ただし、**助動詞がある場合はその助動詞だけが主語の前に置かれる**ことに注意しましょう。

- There is no magnetic field around it, **nor is any electric current flowing through it.**
  （その周囲に磁界はなく、電流もその中を流れていない）
- I don't like to order someone to do something, **nor do** I like to be ordered.
  （誰かに何かをしろと命令するのはいやだし、命令されるのもいやだ）
- He could not complete the assignment in time, **nor could I** (complete the assignment in time).（彼は期限内に課題を仕上げることができなかったが、僕もできなかった）

Once 〜：いったん〜すると

onceは多くの場合、文末や文中で用いられて「一度、一回」と回数を表しますが、文頭で用いられると「**いったん〜すると、一度〜してしまえば**」という接続詞の役割になります。

- **Once** you use the application, you cannot do without it.（そのアプリケーションを一度使うと、それなしではいられなくなりますよ）
- **Once** current flows through the conductor, it also produces magnetic flux around the loop.
  （電流が導体を流れると、輪の回りに磁束を発生させる）

such that 〜：〜というようなもの

ここでのsuchは代名詞で、「そのようなもの」という意味で、実際に「どのようなもの」なのかを後に続くthat節で説明する形になっています。

- The direction of induced current is **such that** it opposes the change of magnetic flux that causes it.（誘導電流の〔流れる〕方向は、それを引き起こす磁力線の変化に対抗するもの〔方向〕になる）
- This experiment is **such that** it is expected to make a new discovery.
  （この実験は新たな発見が期待されているものである）

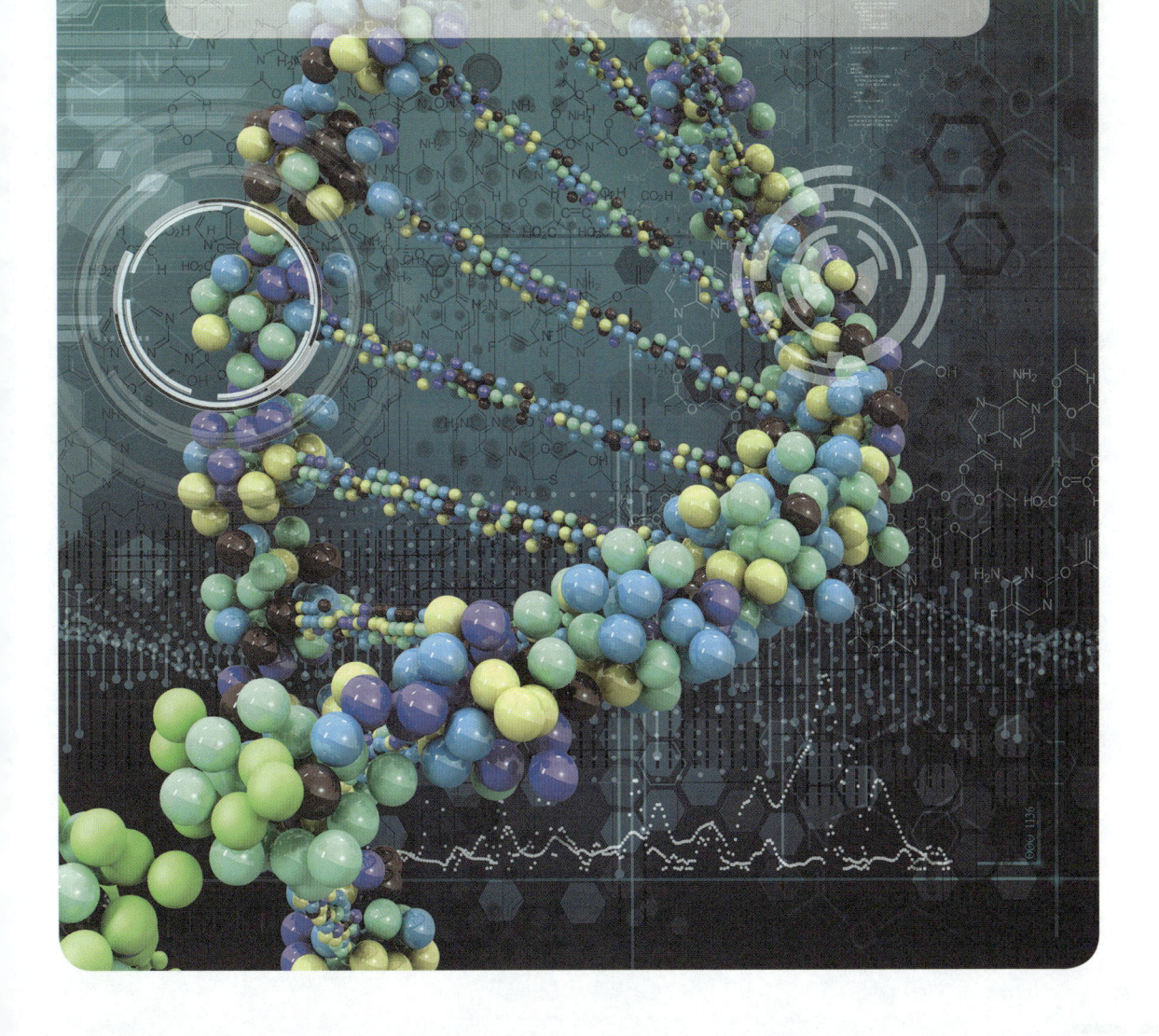

Lesson 8

Cells and Reproduction

Cells

2-32~36

All living things are made up of cells. However, animal cells and plant cells have both common features and different features.

What they have in common are the nucleus,
5 cytoplasm, cell membrane, and mitochondria.

The nucleus contains chromosomes, which carry genetic information. Cell membranes protect the cells and regulate the movement of substances into and out of the cell. Cytoplasm includes all the materials inside the cell
10 and outside of the nucleus. Mitochondria create energy to run the cell. The energy created by mitochondria is converted from glucose through chemical reactions.

Plant cells have some components that animal cells don't have, such as a cell wall, chloroplasts, and a
15 vacuole. The cell wall is a tough and flexible structure situated on the outside of the cell membrane. A vacuole occupies a large amount of the cell volume and it is where nutrients and waste chemicals are stored. Chloroplasts are tiny structures which contain chlorophyll, a green
20 pigment that absorbs light energy for photosynthesis.

membrane [mémbrein]

mitochondria [màitəkándriə]

chromosome [króuməsòum]

genetic [dʒənétik]

regulate [régjəlèit]

convert [kənvə́:rt]

glucose [glú:kous]

chloroplast [klɔ́:rəplæ̀st]

vacuole [vǽkjuòul]

tough [tʌf]

flexible [fléksəbl]

situate [sítʃuèit]

occupy [ákjəpài]

waste [wéist]

chlorophyll [klɔ́(:)rəfil]

pigment [pígmənt]

photosynthesis [fòutousínθəsis]

in common：共通して

Grammar and Expressions

関係副詞whereの先行詞省略　(→ p. 84)

A vacuole occupies a large amount of the cell volume and it is **where** nutrients and waste chemicals are stored.

Practice

A 日本語と同じ意味になるように、（　　）内に適切な語を入れましょう。

1. ほとんどの鉱物は化学的な元素からできている。

   Most minerals (　　　) (　　　) (　　　) of chemical elements.

2. どの方法を使うかを決めるには、それらの相違点に焦点を当てる必要がある。

   To decide (　　) method to employ, we should focus on their (　　) (　　).

3. 若い経営者たちが共通して持っているものは、成功したいという強い願望だ。

   (　　) the young leaders have (　　) (　　) is their strong desire to succeed.

4. 電流を直流から交流に変換する装置をインバータという。

   A device to (　　) electric current (　　) DC (　　) AC is called an inverter.

B 選択肢の動詞を適切な形にして空欄に補いましょう。

1. All goods are accompanied by a tag that (　　　) information on the origin.
2. The pupil (　　　) the amount of light that will enter the eye.
3. The nuclear power plant is (　　　) along the coast.
4. How much electricity will it take to (　　　) the factory?
5. Where are your photos and videos (　　　) on your smartphone?

[store / situate / regulate / carry / run / control]

C 1〜3 に示された各文をもとに、関係詞を用いて日本語と同じ意味の英文を作りましょう。先行詞が省略できる場合は省略しましょう。

1. The hard disk is a device. You can store files and documents there.

   → ハードディスクは、ファイルや文書を収納する装置である。

2. A Control Tower is a place. Air traffic controllers work there.

   → 航空管制塔は、航空管制官が働いている場所です。

3. The small intestine is an organ. Most chemical digestion takes place there.

   → 小腸は、化学的な消化のほとんどが行われる器官である。

Living and Growth of Cells

CD 2-37~40

Organisms that consist of a single cell are called
unicellular organisms. Most unicellular organisms
are of microscopic size. Amoeba, yeast, and euglena
are examples of unicellular organisms. The single cell
5 of a unicellular organism performs all life processes.
It absorbs nutrients, discharges waste, grows, and
reproduces.

Organisms that consist of more than one cell are
called multicellular organisms. Cells of multicellular
10 organisms differentiate and perform specialized functions
to keep their life process continuing.

Whether unicellular or multicellular, all living
things must obtain and use energy to live. They can
either make their own food or depend on others to
15 survive. Green plants produce their own food from
photosynthesis, in which they use energy from sunlight
to convert carbon dioxide and water into glucose
and oxygen. Some of the glucose produced through
photosynthesis is used to provide the energy for growth
20 and reproduction.

unicellular
[jùːniséljulə*r*]

microscopic
[màikrəskápik]

amoeba [əmíːbə]

yeast [jíːst]

euglena [juːglíːnə]

reproduce
[rìːprədúːs]

multicellular
[mʌltiséljulə*r*]

differentiate
[dìfəréniʃèit]

perform [pərfɔ́ːrm]

specialize
[spéʃəlàiz]

obtain [əbtéin]

survive [sərváiv]

growth [gróuθ]

reproduction
[rìːprədʌ́kʃən]

whether A or B：Aであれ Bであれ

Grammar and Expressions

動詞 (keepなど) + 目的語 + 分詞　(→ p. 84)

Cells of multicellular organisms perform specialized functions to **keep** their life process **continuing**.

either A or B (AかBかどちらか)　(→ p. 85)

They can **either** make their own food **or** depend on others to survive.

Practice

A 日本語と同じ意味になるように、（　）内に適切な語を入れましょう。

1. 両地域は、面積と人口の点において似たような大きさだ。
Both regions are (　)(　)(　) in surface area and population.

2. お待たせして申し訳ありません。
I'm so sorry to (　)(　)(　).

3. 国産であれ外国製であれ、車の動力は電気に変わりつつある。
(　) domestic (　) foreign, the power of cars is shifting to electricity.

4. 免疫は、自然にも人為的にも獲得される。
Immunity can be obtained (　) naturally (　) artificially.

5. あなたか彼のどちらかが間違っています。
(　) you (　) he (　) wrong.

6. 北京では私の中国語は通じなかった。
I could not make myself (　) in Chinese in Beijing.

7. 水を出しっぱなしにしないこと。
Don't leave the water (　).

B 選択肢の動詞を適切な形にして空欄に補いましょう。

1. Consumers should (　) types of plastics before they recycle the goods.

2. The first part of the guide (　) the information to install the software.

3. The black-colored body of the device (　) heat efficiently.

4. Help yourself first, not just (　) on others.

[provide / depend / absorb / differentiate / discharge]

Asexual Reproduction

2-41~43

When living things make new cells for growth or repair, they use a type of cell division called mitosis. In mitosis, the chromosomes in the nuclei make identical copies of themselves before dividing. Chromosomes are
5 made of DNA, which is a long molecule in the shape of a double helix. It carries the genetic information in genes. A gene is a section of DNA and it controls the activities of particular cells, such as nerve cells and blood cells. After the chromosomes have been duplicated, the cell splits to
10 create two identical copies of the original cell.

All living things use mitosis to grow and repair themselves, but some use it to reproduce. The offspring reproduced by mitosis need only a single parent, because they are identical copies of their parents. This type of
15 reproduction is called asexual reproduction, or cloning. Some kinds of plants, such as potatoes and strawberries, can reproduce asexually by mitosis.

asexual [eisékʃuəl]

repair [ripéər]

mitosis [maitóusis]

nuclei [núːkliaɪ]

double [dʌ́bl]

helix [híːliks]

gene [dʒíːn]

section [sékʃən]

activity [æktívəti]

duplicate
[dúːplikèit]

split [splít]

offspring
[ɔ́(ː)fspriŋ]

cloning [klóuniŋ]

asexually
[eisékʃuəli]

🔠 Grammar and Expressions

> **再帰代名詞** (→ p. 85)
>
> The chromosomes in the nuclei make identical copies of **themselves** before dividing.
>
> All living things use mitosis to grow and repair **themselves**.

📝 Practice

A 日本語と同じ意味になるように、( ) 内に適切な語を入れましょう。

1. この3Dプリンターで、それらの部品の複製が作れます。

This 3D printer allows you to make ( ) ( ) of those parts.

2. DNAの二重らせん構造は1950年代に発見された。

The ( ) ( ) ( ) of DNA was discovered in 1950s.

3. ハイブリッドとは異種の親から作られた子孫のことである。

A hybrid is the ( ) produced from parents of different species together.

4. クローニングは、農業的に好ましい形質を持つ動植物の複製を作るのに使われる。

( ) is used to make ( ) of plants and animals with desirable agricultural ( ).

B 選択肢の動詞を適切な形にして空欄に補いましょう。

1. Brakes are the main parts in driving to ( ) the speed of cars.

2. The flow of water is ( ) by the valve.

3. The country ( ) into two countries more than fifty years ago.

[split / duplicate / regulate / control]

C 1〜3に示された各文の下線部を主語にして、受動態の文に直しましょう。

1. Once you have placed your order successfully, we will send an email to you.

2. They have developed many nickel alloys with excellent properties.

3. We have identified some potential risk factors of lung cancer.

Sexual Reproduction

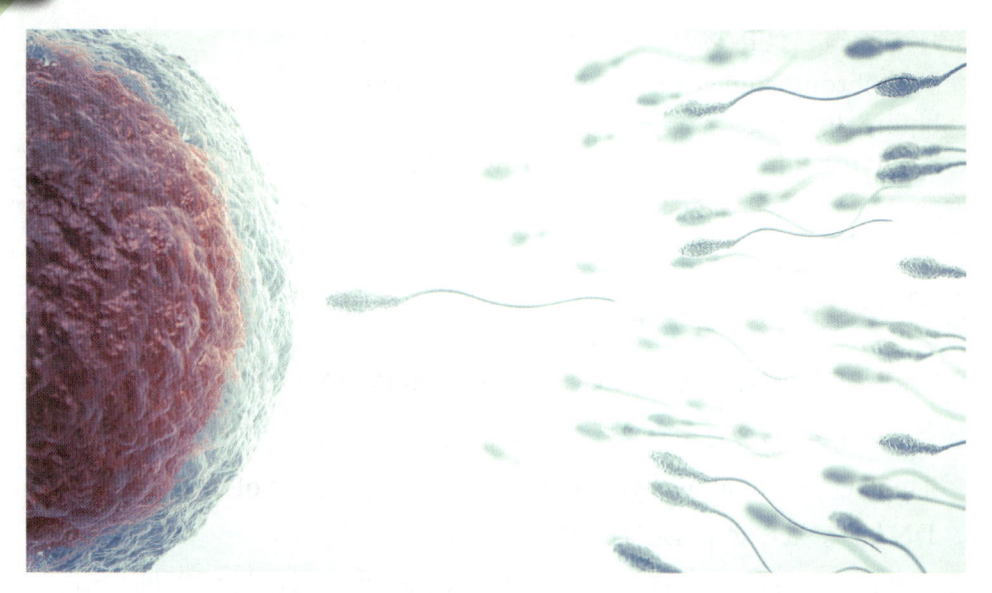

2-44~48

As opposed to asexual reproduction which involves only one parent, sexual reproduction always involves both male and female parents.

During the process of sexual reproduction, sex cells
5 called gametes are produced. The male gamete of an animal is the sperm produced in its testis, and the female gamete is the egg produced in its ovaries.

Sex cells are formed through a special type of cell division called meiosis that halves the number of
10 chromosomes in their parent cells. As a result, the four gametes contain only one set of chromosomes from the original cell. When the two nuclei fuse through fertilization, the fertilized egg has a pair of chromosomes: one from the mother, and the other from the father.
15 Which chromosome comes from each pair is completely random.

Plants also reproduce through sexual reproduction. The male gametes are produced in the anthers of the stamens, and the female gametes are produced in the
20 ovary. In order for fertilization to occur, pollination must happen. The pollen of plants is transferred from the anther to the stigma by insects, wind and so on.

sexual [sékʃuəl]

involve [inválv]

gamete [gəmíːt]

sperm [spə́ːrm]

testis [téstis]

ovary [óuvəri]

meiosis [maióusis]

fuse [fjúːz]

fertilization [fə̀ːrtəlizéiʃən]

fertilize [fə́ːrtəlàiz]

completely [kəmplíːtli]

anther [ǽnθər]

stamen [stéimən]

pollination [pàːlənéiʃən]

pollen [pálən]

stigma [stígmə]

insect [ínsekt]

Grammar and Expressions

> in order for ～ to ... (→ p. 85)
>
> **In order for** fertilization **to** occur, pollination must happen.

Practice

Ⓐ 日本語と同じ意味になるように、（　　）内に適切な語を入れましょう。

1. オゾンは酸素の化学反応を通して形成される。

   Ozone is (　　　) (　　　) chemical reactions of oxygen.

2. ある決まった量の気体圧力を2倍にすると、その体積は半分になる。

   If you (　　) the pressure on a given amount of gas, its volume will (　　).

Ⓑ 日本語と同じ意味になるように、[　　]内の語句を並べ替えて言ってみましょう。

1. その3色の中でどの色が一番お好きですか。

   [best / color / do / like / of / the / the three / which / you]?

2. 私はコンピューターサイエンスのどの研究分野を選ぶべきでしょうか。

   [choose / computer science / I / in / research area / should / which]?

3. どの方法で支払えますか。クレジットカード払いのみです。

   [accept / do / methods / payment / of / which / you]? – We only accept credit cards.

Ⓒ 例にならって、各文を不定詞を使って書き換えましょう。

   例：Pollination must happen so that fertilization can occur.

   → In order for fertilization to occur, pollination must happen

1. Small companies must change through technological innovations so that they can remain competitive.

   → ＿＿＿＿＿＿＿＿＿＿＿＿＿＿＿＿＿＿＿, they must change through technological innovations.

2. The alloy needs to contain more chromium so that it might be categorized as a stainless steel.

   → ＿＿＿＿＿＿＿＿＿＿＿＿＿＿＿＿＿＿＿, it needs to contain more chromium.

3. We need hundreds of volunteers so that our event will be a success.

   → ＿＿＿＿＿＿＿＿＿＿＿＿＿＿＿＿＿＿＿, we need hundreds of volunteers.

関係副詞whereの先行詞省略

関係副詞の **where** は、関係代名詞と同様、先行詞（名詞）を後置修飾します。ただし、先行詞が場所を表すことが明確な場合は省略されることがあります。**where** に限らず、他の関係副詞 **when** や **why** も同様で、**when** の先行詞は「時」を、**why** の先行詞は「理由」を表すことが、ある程度明確だからです。関係代名詞では通常このようなことは起こりません（先行詞のない関係代名詞である **what** だけは例外 → p. viii 参照）。

- A vacuole is **where** nutrients and waste chemicals are stored.
  （液胞とは、栄養と老廃物が貯蔵されるところです）
- That's **where** the students are mistaken.
  （そこが学生たちの間違っている点だ）
- The most exciting part of the movie is **where** the hero breaks the hidden code.（その映画の最も面白いところは、主人公が隠された暗号を解くところだ）
- I remember **when** I lived in a dormitory.
  （学生寮に住んでいたときのことを覚えています）
- That is **why** I told you not to go alone.
  （だから一人で行くなと言ったんだよ）

動詞（keepなど）+ 目的語 + 分詞

SVOCの中のC（補語）として、分詞が使われる場合があります。補語が現在分詞か過去分詞かは、文中の目的語と補語の関係で決まります。この型の動詞には **keep**, **leave**, **find**, **want**, **catch** などがあります。

- Cells of multicellular organisms <u>keep</u> their life process <u>continuing</u>.
  （多細胞生物の細胞は、その生命を維持する） ◀ … [their life process (is) continuing]. なので能動の関係にある
- Someone <u>left</u> the printer <u>broken</u>.（誰かがプリンターを壊れたまま放置した） ◀ Someone left [the printer (was) broken]. なので受動の関係にある

either A or B (AかBかどちらか)

either A or BのAとBには同じ品詞の語か、同じはたらきの句や節が来ます。

- They can **either** make their own food **or** depend on others to live.（かれらは自分たちで食料を作るか、他者に依存して生きることができる）
- **Either** I forgot to tell him **or** he was not listening.
  （私が彼に言い忘れたか、彼が聞いていなかったかだ）

また、**either A or B**が主語のとき、それに続く動詞の人称や数は、Bに合わせるのが普通です。

- **Either** you **or** he **has** to do it.
  （あなたか彼のどちらかがそれをやらなければならない）

再帰代名詞

「～自身」という意味を表す人称代名詞を再帰代名詞といいます。**myself**, **yourself**, **himself**, **herself**などがあり、辞書等にはこれらの一般形である**oneself**という形で載っています。動詞や前置詞の目的語になり、動詞の場合は、自分の行為が自分に対してなされる場合に使われます。

- The chromosomes in the nuclei make identical copies of **themselves** before dividing.
  （核の中の染色体は、分裂の前に自分自身と同一のコピーを作る）
- All living things use mitosis to grow and repair **themselves**.（全ての生き物は有糸分裂を使って自分自身を成長させたり修復したりする）

in order for ～ to…

in order to ～のような、to不定詞が含まれるイディオムの中で、意味上の主語が必要な場合は、**for ～**を**to …**の前に置きます（→ p. 51　to不定詞の意味上の主語 参照）。

- **In order for** this program **to** work, we all have to do our best.（このプログラムを機能させるためには、我々がんばらなければならない）
- **In order for** fertilization **to** occur, pollination must happen.
  （受精が起こるには、授粉が起こらなければならない）
- That question is easy **enough for** children **to** answer.
  （その質問は子供でも答えられるくらい簡単だ）
- The luggage is **too** heavy **for** me **to** carry.
  （その荷物は私には重すぎて運べない）

Let's read!

2012 年のノーベル賞受賞で広く知られるようになった iPS 細胞。あらゆる細胞に変化する能力を持つ iPS 細胞は、どのように役立てられるのでしょうか。

Q What are iPS cells likely to be utilized?

A It is thought that iPS cells will be useful in elucidating the causes of disease, developing new drugs, and in cell transplantation therapy and other forms of regenerative medicine. Regenerative medicine is a therapy aimed at restoring functions lost through disease or injury. Regenerative medicine in the case of diabetes mellitus, for example, involves transplanting cells with the ability to regulate blood sugar level, or in the case of traumas where nerves have become severed, transplanting nerve cells that can help restore the interrupted connection. iPS cells could be used to make these transplanted cells.

Meanwhile, by generating iPS cells from the somatic cells of patients with intractable diseases and inducing them to differentiate into the cells of the diseased tissue, we hope to enable research to elucidate the causes of the respective disease. One example is diseases which arise due to changes in the brain, as brain cells are extremely difficult to acquire and study from live patients. Using iPS cells, researchers hope to compare healthy and diseased cells.

iPS cells will also make it possible to evaluate and test pharmaceutical efficacy, side effects, and toxicity in a way not possible in the human body, which should give a great impetus to new drug development. Once safety has been ensured, we can additionally look forward to applications in regenerative medicine, including cell transplantation therapy involving transplantation of tissue and organ cells created by differentiation from patient-derived iPS cells.

出典：京都大学 iPS 細胞研究所 CiRA（https://www.cira.kyoto-u.ac.jp/e/faq/faq_ips.html）

Lesson 9

Chemical Reactions

Combination and Decomposition

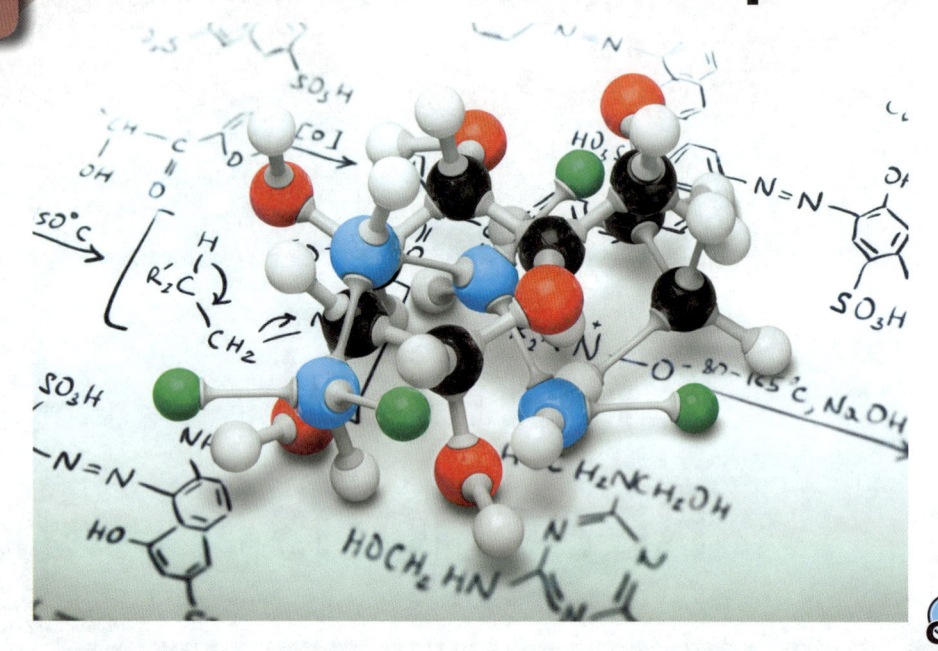

2-49~53

A chemical reaction is a process in which one or
more substances are converted to one or more different
substances. The substances that react together are called
the reactants, and the substances that are formed as a
5 result of the reaction are called the products.

Reactants and products are either chemical
elements or compounds. The atoms in a compound are
chemically combined by strong forces called bonds. This
makes the properties of a compound different from the
10 elements it contains.

One of the major chemical reactions is a combination
reaction, where two or more reactants combine to form
a single product. When a combination reaction is used
to produce a desired product, that process is called the
15 synthesis of that product. Synthesis can result in the
formation of more than one product. Many materials are
synthesized from chemicals derived from various sources.

Another major chemical reaction is decomposition,
where a substance splits into two or more simpler
20 substances. In some cases, the reactant breaks down into
its component elements, and in other cases, they may
break down into smaller molecules.

combination
[kàmbənéiʃən]

decomposition
[dì:kampəzíʃən]

reactant [riæktənt]

desire [dizáiər]

synthesis [sínθəsis]

formation
[fɔːrméiʃən]

synthesize
[sínθəsàiz]

derive [diráiv]

Reading Comprehension

本文の内容に合うように（　　）内に適切な語を入れましょう。

1. (　　　) are substances that change into other substances through chemical reaction.
2. (　　　) are substances that are formed as a result of chemical reaction.
3. The (　　) of a compound are different from those of the elements it contains.
4. (　　) and (　　) are examples of major chemical reactions.
5. The process of chemical reactions to produce a desirable material is called (　　).

Practice

A 日本語と同じ意味になるように、（　　）内に適切な語を入れましょう。

1. 化学反応とは、そこで一つあるいは複数の物質が他の物質に変換されるプロセスである。
   A chemical reaction is a (　　) in (　　) one or more substances are (　　) into different substances.
2. 反応物と生成物は化学的な元素か化合物のどちらかである。
   Reactants and products are either chemical (　　) or (　　).
3. 様々な原料に由来する化学物質から多くの物質が合成される。
   Many materials are (　　) from chemicals (　　) from various sources.
4. 分解反応によって、物質は二つ以上のより単純な物質に分かれる。
   Through a (　　) reaction, a substance splits into (　　) (　　) (　　) simpler substances.

B 日本語と同じ意味になるように、[　　]内の語句を並べ替えて言ってみましょう。

1. 元素を互いに違うものにしているのは何ですか。
   [different / each / elements / from / makes / other / what]?
2. どの酵素がデンプンを糖に分解するのに使われるのですか。
   [break / down / enzyme / into / is / starch / sugar / to / used / which]?
3. 整備不良は重大な事故を引き起こす故障につながる場合があります。
   Improper maintenance may [trouble / accidents / causing / in / result / serious].

Part 2 Oxidation and Reduction

2-54~57

Oxidation is the reaction of a substance with oxygen or the addition of oxygen to a substance in a reaction. Reduction, on the other hand, is the reaction of the removal of oxygen from a substance. Oxidation and
5 reduction always occur at the same time. The set of these reactions is called the oxidation-reduction reaction, or redox reaction for short.

Let's take an example. When you heat copper in air at around 300 to 800°C, the copper reacts with oxygen
10 and a black material called copper(II) oxide is formed. This is an oxidation reaction. Then when you heat the copper(II) oxide in hydrogen gas, the hydrogen combines with the oxygen of the copper(II) oxide and produces water, with copper metal remaining. This process is
15 reduction.

Oxidation and reduction can also be explained in terms of electrons. In case of the redox reaction of copper(II) oxide in terms of electron transfer, copper loses electrons and the electrons that copper loses are accepted
20 by the oxygen. In this case, the copper is oxidized, and the oxygen is reduced. In other words, oxidation is a loss of electrons and reduction is a gain of electrons.

oxidation [ὰksidéiʃən]
reduction [ridʌ́kʃən]
removal [rimúːvəl]
redox [ríːdɑks]
oxide [ὰksaid]
explain [ikspléin]
accept [əksépt]
oxidize [ὰksədàiz]
reduce [ridúːs]
loss [lɔ́(ː)s]

copper(II) oxide：酸化銅（II）

📖 Reading Comprehension

本文の内容に合うように（　　）内に適切な語を入れましょう。

1. Oxidation can be explained as (　　　) of oxygen to a substance as well as a (　　　) of electrons.

2. Reduction can be explained as (　　　) of oxygen from a substance as well as a (　　　) of electrons.

3. The set of oxidation reaction and reduction reaction is called (　　　) for short.

4. Copper(II) oxide is formed when the copper is heated in (　　　) at a (　　　) temperature.

5. When the copper(II) oxide is heated in (　　　) gas, (　　　) copper and water are produced.

📝 Practice

Ⓐ （　　）内に入る適切な語句を選択肢から選び意味を言いましょう。

1. A body above the ground has potential energy. (　　　), it has stored energy due to its position.

2. (　　　) culture, European countries are completely different from America.

3. (　　　) nuclear accident, large numbers of people will have to migrate to other places.

4. Learning is not boring. (　　　), learning something new can be one of the most enjoyable activities.

5. Natto, (　　　) fermented whole soybeans is a traditional food of Japan.

[on the contrary / in terms of / in case of / in other words / or]

Ⓑ 日本語と同じ意味になるように、付帯状況を表す with を使って1文にしましょう。

1. Our district still has five teams that could win the title. Four games remain.
4試合を残し、当地区には優勝する可能性のあるチームがまだ5つある。

2. The city's growth has been accelerating. Its population has increased 20 percent in the last decade.
その都市の成長は加速し続けており、この10年間に20パーセント人口が増えた。

Oxidizing Agents and Reducing Agents

2-58~63

Oxidation and reduction as loss and gain of electrons between the substances can explain reactions in which oxygen is not involved.

Let's look at the example of the redox reaction of
5 copper(II) sulfate, which consists of copper and sulfate instead of oxygen. When we place a zinc plate into a solution of copper(II) sulfate, both copper and sulfate exist as ions. Then, zinc metal displaces copper ions, producing copper metal and a solution of zinc sulfate.

10 You see that the zinc atoms have lost electrons and have formed positively charged zinc ions. At the same time, when the zinc atoms have been oxidized, the zinc atoms have reduced the copper ions.

In a redox reaction, the substance which donates the
15 electrons to another element or ions is called a reducing agent. Alkali metals are the strongest reducing agents because they lose electrons very easily. The substance which accepts the electrons is called an oxidizing agent. Common oxidizing agents are oxygen, hydrogen peroxide,
20 and the halogens.

In the example of the redox reaction of copper(II) sulfate above, zinc is the reducing agent and copper is the oxidizing agent.

zinc [zíŋk]

displace [displéis]

donate [dóuneit]

agent [éidʒənt]

peroxide [pəráksaid]

halogen [hǽlədʒən]

······

sulfate：硫酸塩　**copper(II) sulfate**：硫酸銅（II）　**zinc sulfate**：硫酸亜鉛

📖 Reading Comprehension

本文の内容に合うように（　　）内に適切な語を入れましょう。

1. (　　)(　　) can explain reactions between substances which do not involve oxygen.

2. A (　　) agent is a substance that (　　) an electron to another substance in a redox reaction.

3. An (　　) agent is a substance that (　　) an electron from another substance in a redox reaction.

4. In a copper(II) sulfate solution with a zinc plate in it, the zinc becomes (　　) charged (　　) and the copper becomes the (　　)(　　), respectively.

📝 Practice

A 日本語と同じ意味になるように、選択肢から適切な語句を選び、（　　）内に入れましょう。

> アルカリ金属の還元力が強い理由は、それらが最外殻に電子を1個だけ持っているためである。一つしかない最外殻電子は非常に簡単に他の物質の原子に与えられる。つまり、アルカリ金属はみずからを簡単に酸化し、反応性が高いということである。従って、アルカリ金属は優れた還元剤として機能する。

The reason (1) the alkali metals have high (2) power is that they have one electron in their outermost shell. The only one electron in the outermost shell is very easy to (3) to atoms of another substance. This means that the alkaline metals (4) themselves easily, (5) means that they are highly reactive. Therefore, the alkaline metals act as good reducing agents.

[be donated / be stored / oxidize / reduce / reducing / which / why]

B 日本語の意味になるように [　　] 内の語句を並べ替えましょう。

1. 約0.9パーセントの塩化ナトリウム水溶液は生理食塩水と呼ばれる。
   [0.9 percent / an / approximately / called / is / of / sodium chloride / solution] physiological saline solution.

2. 二酸化硫黄や窒素酸化物のような化合物が空気中に放出されると、酸性雨の原因となる。
   Acid rain is caused when [and / are / into / like / compounds / sulfur dioxide / nitrogen oxides / released / the air].

Lesson 10

Weather

Part 1

Water Vapor

2-64~67

You may have seen the droplets of water on the surface of a cold glass in a warm room. Clouds in the sky form by the same mechanism.

The water droplets on the surface of the glass come
5 from the water vapor in the air. When the glass cools the air around it, the air becomes saturated with water vapor. At that time, the air is holding the maximum amount of water vapor possible. This amount is called the amount of saturated vapor, which depends on the
10 temperature. Once the temperature of the air goes down, the water vapor begins to condense into liquid water. The temperature at which the condensation of water vapor begins is called the dew point.

When warm and moist air rises up into the sky,
15 it expands and cools. When the temperature of the air reaches the saturation point, the water vapor condenses to form tiny water droplets, which develop into clouds. Once the droplets in the clouds grow large and heavy enough, they come down to the ground as precipitation
20 such as rain, snow and so on.

droplet [dróplit]

mechanism [mékənìzm]

saturated [sǽtʃərèitid]

condense [kəndéns]

condensation [kàndenséiʃən]

dew [d(j)úː]

moist [mɔ́ist]

expand [ikspǽnd]

saturation [sǽtʃəréiʃən]

precipitation [prisìpətéiʃən]

📖 Reading Comprehension

本文の内容に合うように（　　）内に適切な語を入れましょう。

1. When the air becomes (　　　　), it can hold the maximum amount of
   (　　　) (　　　) possible.
2. The amount of saturated vapor (　　　) (　　　) temperature.
3. The temperature at which the condensation of water vapor begins is called
   the (　　　) (　　　).
4. Clouds form when the water vapor in the air (　　　) (　　　) water
   droplets.
5. (　　　) is water released from clouds mostly in the form of (　　　).

📝 Practice

A 日本語と同じ意味になるように、[　　] 内の語句を並べ替えて言ってみましょう。

1. なぜ水は油の中だと水滴になるのですか。
   [does / droplets / form / in / oil / water / why]?
2. 沸点とは、液体が気体に変化する温度です。
   The boiling point is [at / a gas / a liquid / changes / into / the temperature /
   which].
3. 幹細胞はどんな種類の細胞にもなることができます。
   Stem cells [any / can / cells / develop / into / kind / of].
4. コンデンサーは気体を液体へと凝縮するために使われる装置です。
   A condenser is [a / condense / device / into / liquids / to / used / gases].

B 日本語と同じ意味になるよう、空欄に適切な語句を補いましょう。

1. あなたは以前に履歴書を書いたことがあるかもしれません。
   You (　　　) (　　　) (　　　) a résumé before.
2. この鉄パイプでそのサイズのテントを支えるには、強度が不十分です。
   This iron pipe is (　　　) (　　　) (　　　) to support the tent of that size.
3. 都市化とは、それによって農村が都市へと成長する過程である。
   Urbanization is the process (　　　) (　　　) rural communities grow to
   form cities.
4. 蒸気エンジン内では、膨張する水蒸気がピストンを押します。
   In a steam engine, (　　　) (　　　) (　　　) pushes a piston.

97

Foehn Phenomenon

CD
2-68~71

When a parcel of warm air lifts up along the windward side of a mountain, it cools as it rises and makes clouds form. Then the clouds cause precipitation which falls on the windward slope and at the summit.

5 Therefore, at the time the air reaches the ridge or the summit, it has already been stripped of most of its moisture. When the already dry air goes down the leeward side of the mountain, it warms again and causes clouds to disappear.

10 If unsaturated air rises, the temperature decreases by 1°C for every 100 meters the air rises. However, once the air has already become saturated, its temperature decreases by 0.5°C as the air rises. When the air sinks, it warms by 1°C per 100 meters.

15 If a parcel of saturated air at 20°C rises up along the slope of a mountain which is 2,000 meters high, it will cool to 10°C once it has risen 2,000 meters. After passing the ridge and descending along the leeward side, it will warm to 30°C, which is much warmer than the original

20 air. This is called the foehn phenomenon.

parcel [páːrsl]

windward [wíndwərd]

mountain [máuntn]

summit [sʌ́mit]

ridge [rídʒ]

strip [stríp]

moisture [mɔ́istʃər]

leeward [líːwərd]

disappear [dìsəpíər]

unsaturated [ʌnsǽtʃərèitid]

descend [disénd]

foehn phenomenon：フェーン現象

98

📖 Reading Comprehension

本文の内容に合うように（　　）内に適切な語を入れましょう。

1. Warm air (　　　　) as it rises up the side of a mountain.

2. The cooler air makes (　　　　) form, which causes precipitation to (　　　　) on the slope.

3. The warm air that has reached the summit of a mountain has already (　　　　) most of its moisture.

4. The temperature of (　　　　) air decreases by 1℃ per 100 meters as it rises up a mountain.

5. The temperature of (　　　　) air decreases by 0.5℃ per 100 meters as it rises up a mountain.

6. The temperature of air increases by 1℃ per 100 meters as it (　　　　) the mountain side.

📝 Practice

Ⓐ 日本語と同じ意味になるように、[　　] 内の語句を並べ替えて言ってみましょう。

1. 水位がそのダムの最大貯水容量に達した。

    [limit / reached / storage / of / the / the dam / the water level].

2. 彼女は、日本語は思っていたよりずっと難しいと言っている。

    She says that [difficult / is / Japanese / more / much / she / than / thought].

3. 衣類についたシミの取り方を知りたいです。

    I'd like to know [clothing / disappear / make / how / on / stains / to].

Ⓑ 日本語と同じ意味になるよう、空欄に適切な語句を補いましょう。

1. 風は風上側から建物の中に入り、風下側から建物を出て行く。

    The wind enters a building on the (　　　　) side and exits on the (　　　　) side.

2. 台風で木の葉がみんな落ちた。

    The typhoon (　　　　) the trees (　　　　) all their leaves.

3. スコアを降順に並べなさい。

    Arrange scores in (　　　　) (　　　　).

4. 飽和していない空気のかたまりは100メートルごとに1度ずつ温度が下がる。

    A parcel of (　　　　) air cools by 1℃ every 100 meters.

Wind

2-72~75

The wind blows from areas where the atmospheric pressure is higher to where it is lower. When warm air rises, cooler air will replace it. This causes a horizontal air flow, which is wind.

5   Observed on a global scale, winds do not blow in a straight line. This is because the earth is rotating. In the northern hemisphere, the spin of the earth causes winds to curve to the right. Therefore, winds blow clockwise around an area of high pressure and counter-clockwise

10 around low pressure. In the southern hemisphere, winds curve in the opposite direction from those in the northern hemisphere for the same reason.

Atmospheric pressure is measured in hectopascals (hPa). Standard pressure at sea level is defined as

15 1013 hPa. Either high or low areas on the weather chart are all relative to each other. In other words, what defines a "high" or a "low" depends on the area around

20 it. Areas of high and low pressure are respectively caused by descending and ascending air. High-pressure systems tend to lead to dry and fine weather, and low-pressure systems often lead to

25 unsettled weather.

blow [blóu]

atmospheric [ætməsférik]

global [glóubəl]

rotate [róuteit]

northern [nɔ́:rðərn]

hemisphere [hémisfiər]

clockwise [klákwàiz]

counter-clockwise [káuntər klákwàiz]

southern [sʌ́ðərn]

standard [stǽndərd]

relative [rélətiv]

ascend [əsénd]

tend [ténd]

unsettled [ʌnsétld]

📖 Reading Comprehension

本文の内容に合うように（　　）内に適切な語を入れましょう。

1. Wind is a (　　　) flow of air caused by differences in the (　　　) (　　　).
2. A (　　　) (　　　) means that the atmospheric pressure of a region is lower than the surrounding area.
3. Regions under a (　　　) (　　　) usually experience good weather.

📝 Practice

Ⓐ　日本語と同じ意味になるように、[　　]内の語句を並べ替えて言ってみましょう。

1. このアプリケーションはあなたがいる場所から行きたい場所までの最適なルートを教えてくれます。
   This application tells you the best routes [are / from / go / where / to / to / want / where / you / you].
2. 丘の上から見ると、その街の夜景は言葉で表現できないほど美しかった。
   [from / of / seen / the hill / the top], the night view of the city was [beautiful / could / describe / it / no words / so / that].
3. 摩擦は、その物体の表面がどれだけ滑らかであるかということによって変わる。
   Friction [depends / how / is / of / on / smooth / the object / the surface].

Ⓑ　日本語と同じ意味になるよう、空欄に適切な語句を補いましょう。

1. このリフトで、階段を使わずに昇り降りができます。
   This lift lets you (　　　) and (　　　) without stairs.
2. 地球は太陽の周りを公転しながら、地軸を中心に自転している。
   The Earth (　　　) on its (　　　), orbiting around the Sun.
3. 人生における成功とは何かについての定義は人それぞれだ。
   Everyone has a different (　　　) of (　　　) success in his life is.
4. フラストレーションは不安定な行動につながるおそれがあると言われている。
   It is said that frustration may (　　　) to (　　　) behavior.
5. 幸福と感じるか不幸と感じるかは互いに相対的なものである。
   Feeling happy or unhappy is (　　　) to (　　　) (　　　).

Word List

Words	ページ	COCET 2600
A		
acceleration	22	1031
accept	90	1027
accurately	32	
activity	80	249
adjacent	2	2511
advance	58	946
affect	54	874
aftershock	56	
agency	58	827
agent	92	827
alert	58	1555
amoeba	78	
amount	16	498
amplitude	44	1313
analyze	58	1152
angle	2	131
anther	82	
antiderivative	36	
apparent	46	1749
appear	26	954
apply	68	769
approximate	16	
approximately	26	1087
arbitrary	4	2510
arc	4	1147
archipelago	60	
arrange	12	1891

Words	ページ	COCET 2600
arrival	58	
arrowed	66	
ascend	100	2370
asexual	80	
asexually	80	
atmospheric	100	
atomic	12	738
attract	26	1307
average	22	507
axis	6	500
B		
balanced	24	
bend	60	1896
blow	100	1471
boundary	60	1572
C		
calculate	22	1034
calculus	34	
catastrophic	54	
certain	12	506
chemically	12	
chemistry	16	449
chlorophyll	76	1327
chloroplast	76	
chromosome	76	1457
circumference	4	1146
clockwise	100	1436

Words	ページ	COCET 2600	Words	ページ	COCET 2600
emergency	58	1226	frequency	44	905
emit	14	1165	frequent	54	904
entire	4	1296	function	2	1139
epicenter	54		fundamental	12	1386
equation	24	493	further	54	526
euglena	78		fuse	82	
exact	16	1176			

Words	ページ	COCET 2600
	G	
gamete	82	
gas	16	91
gene	80	642
genetic	76	642
global	100	316
glucose	76	1325
gradient	22	2412
graphically	66	
gravitation	26	
gravitational	26	1320
gravity	26	1320
grip	66	181
growth	78	853

Words	ページ	COCET 2600
except	36	351
exert	26	1032
exist	14	730
expand	96	1044
experience	54	821
explain	90	459
exponent	34	
express	4	1532
external	68	1609

Words	ページ	COCET 2600
	F	
fault	58	1339
fertilization	82	
fertilize	82	1458
field	66	377
figure	4	494
flexible	76	2137
flux	66	
focus	54	1012
force	24	440
foreshock	56	
formation	88	1599
formula	24	1379

Words	ページ	COCET 2600
	H	
halogen	92	
helix	80	
hemisphere	100	1380
hence	34	
hertz	44	
horizontal	22	2040
hypotenuse	2	

Words	ページ	COCET 2600
mole	16	
molecule	16	739
monomial	34	
motion	22	146
mountain	98	
movement	24	802
multicellular	78	

	N	
nanometer	48	
neutron	12	1356
nor	70	
northern	100	474
nuclei	80	
nucleus	12	1358

	O	
observe	46	950
obtain	78	1360
occupy	76	1904
offspring	80	1879
oppose	70	837
opposite	2	481
origin	6	317
oscillate	42	
ovary	82	
oxidation	90	990
oxide	90	990
oxidize	90	990

	P	
parcel	98	1654

Words	ページ	COCET 2600
particle	12	1001
perform	78	1299
periodically	44	
peroxide	92	
perpendicular	42	2039
phenomenon	46	1322
photosynthesis	76	1328
phrase	2	2126
pigment	76	1329
pitch	46	2187
plane	6	
plug	46	276
pole	66	717
pollen	82	1927
pollination	82	
polynomial	34	
portion	4	2287
possess	14	2265
possibility	58	910
power	36	19
precede	56	2497
precipitation	96	2599
predict	54	949
preliminary	56	2100
primary	56	2017
prime	34	785
principal	56	2045
process	34	622
product	26	486
propagate	44	
propagation	42	
property	12	1052

Words	ページ	COCET 2600		Words	ページ	COCET 2600
proportional	26	325		relative	100	1183
proton	12	1357		remain	24	391
pull	24	183		removal	90	
pulse	44	1057		repair	80	1692
push	24	182		represent	44	1043
				reproduce	78	1832

				reproduction	78	
Q				resistance	24	436

quadratic	32			respect	36	1418
quantity	22	909		respectively	12	1438
				respond	48	886

				responsible	60	1397
R				resultant	24	

radian	4			retreat	46	2267
radiation	14	863		reverse	36	179
radio	48			ridge	98	2173
radioisotope	14			rotate	100	1461

radius	4	1145				
range	56	437		**S**		

rate	22	709		saturated	96	
reach	6	460		saturation	96	2235
react	12	762		scalar	22	
reactant	88			scale	26	907
rebound	60			secant	32	
redefine	16			secondary	56	2018
redox	90			section	80	1265
reduce	90	532		seismic	54	2135
reduction	90	532		seismometer	58	
refract	48			sexual	82	1445
refractive	48			shake	54	275
regardless	16	1439		shallow	58	580
regulate	76			shape	6	577
relate	16	1036				
relationship	2	1140				

Words	ページ	COCET 2600
shell	60	1491
shockwave	56	
sine	2	
site	58	677
situate	76	
slope	22	1132
solenoid	68	
somehow	12	956
source	46	747
southern	100	475
specialize	78	846
specific	12	1180
specify	2	1180
spectrum	48	1391
sperm	82	1455
split	80	1496
spring	42	
stable	14	1611
stamen	82	
standard	100	711
state	16	372
stationary	22	2387
steep	22	1258
stigma	82	
string	44	1723
strip	98	1698
structure	60	712
subduction	60	
substance	12	539
subtend	4	

Words	ページ	COCET 2600
suffer	54	839
sum	34	1381
summit	98	1343
suppose	46	562
surround	36	1166
survive	78	885
swing	42	278
symbolize	16	
synthesis	88	2024
synthesize	88	2024

T

Words	ページ	COCET 2600
tangent	2	
tectonic	60	
tend	100	1109
term	56	674
testis	82	
theta	2	
thick	60	596
thumb	66	1061
tough	76	1792
toward	6	342
transfer	42	1164
transform	14	1368
transverse	42	
travel	22	
tremor	56	
trigonometry	2	
trough	44	

Words	ページ	COCET 2600
U		
unbalanced	24	
underneath	60	349
unicellular	78	
universal	26	2139
universe	14	683
unsaturated	98	
unsettled	100	
unstable	14	1611
V		
vacuole	76	
vacuum	48	688
value	6	497
vary	54	1035
vector	22	1143
velocity	22	1321
vertical	44	2039
visible	48	1291
volcano	60	1868
W		
warning	54	878
warp	60	
waste	76	757
wavelength	44	1312
weight	16	555
whole	42	307
wind	68	210
windward	98	
within	68	

Words	ページ	COCET 2600
X		
x-ray	48	862
Y		
yeast	78	
Z		
zinc	92	1737
zone	60	1682

TEXT PRODUCTION STAFF

edited by / 編集	
Eiichi Tamura	田村 栄一
Mitsugu Shishido	宍戸 貢

English-language editing by / 英文校閲	
Bill Benfield	ビル・ベンフィールド
Walter Kasmer	ウォルター・カズマ

cover design by / 表紙デザイン	
sein	ザイン

text design by / 本文デザイン	
sein	ザイン

CD PRODUCTION STAFF

narrated by / 吹込み者	
Josh Keller (AmE)	ジョシュ・ケラー (アメリカ英語)
Rachel Walzer (AmE)	レイチェル・ウォルツァー (アメリカ英語)

Fundamental Science in English II
理工系学生のための基礎英語II

2019年1月20日　初版発行
2024年1月25日　第 5 刷発行

著　　者　亀山太一　青山晶子　武田淳

Workbook　石貫文子　井上英俊　大森誠　紙谷智　佐竹直喜　菅原崇
執 筆 者　瀬川直美　高越義一　種村俊介　服部真弓　藤田卓郎　前田哲宏
　　　　　宮本友紀　森和憲

発 行 者　佐野 英一郎

発 行 所　株式会社 成 美 堂
　　　　　〒101-0052　東京都千代田区神田小川町3-22
　　　　　TEL 03-3291-2261　FAX 03-3293-5490
　　　　　https://www.seibido.co.jp

印 刷・製 本　(株)加藤文明社

ISBN 978-4-7919-7195-4　　　　　　　　　　　　　Printed in Japan

● 数学の数式と読み方

階乗 (factorial)

n!	n factorial

和分記号 (summation notation)

$\displaystyle\sum_{i=1}^{n} ui$	the sum of all the terms ui from i equals 1 to n.

定積分 (definite integral)

$\displaystyle\int_{a}^{b} f(x)dx$	the integral from a to b of f of $x\, dx$

ピタゴラスの定理 (Pythagorean theorem)

$a^2 + b^2 = c^2$	a squared plus b squared equals c squared.

オイラーの公式 (Euler's Formula)

$e^{ix} = \cos x + i \sin x$	e to the (power of) ix equals cosine x plus i sine x.

テイラー展開 (Taylor expansion)

$e^x = 1 + \dfrac{x}{1!} + \dfrac{x^2}{2!} + \dfrac{x^3}{3!} + \cdots,$	e to the (power of) x equals 1 plus x over 1 factorial plus x squared over 2 factorial plus x cubed over 3 factorial and so on.

テイラー級数 (Taylor series)

$f(x) = \displaystyle\sum_{n=0}^{\infty} \dfrac{f^{(n)}(a)}{n!}(x-a)^n$	f of x equals the sum of all the terms the nth derivative f of a over n factorial times x minus a parentheses to the (power of) n from n equals zero to infinitive.

フーリエ級数 (Fourier series)

$f(x) = a_0 + \displaystyle\sum_{n=1}^{\infty}\left(a_n \cos\dfrac{n\pi x}{L} + b_n \sin\dfrac{n\pi x}{L}\right)$	f of x equals a sub zero plus the sum of all the terms a sub n times cosine $n\pi x$ over L plus b sub n sine $n\pi x$ over L from n quals 1 to infinitive.

二項定理 (Binomial theorem)

$(x + a)^n = \displaystyle\sum_{k=0}^{n} \binom{n}{k} x^k a^{n-k}$	x plus a in parentheses to the (power of) n equals the sum of all the terms n combination k times x to the (power of) k times a to the power of n minus k.

ド・モアブルの定理 (de Moivre's theorem)

$\cos n\theta + i \sin n\theta = (\cos\theta + i\sin\theta)^n = e^{\sin\theta}$	cosine $n\theta$ plus i sine $n\theta$ equals cosine θ plus i sine θ equals e to the (power of) sine θ